A SINGLE REVOLUTION

A Single Revolution

DON'T LOOK FOR A MATCH.
LIGHT ONE.

Shani Silver

Atta Girl

P R E S S

A SINGLE REVOLUTION
Don't look for a match. Light one.

ISBN   978-1-5445-2531-0   *Hardcover*
       978-1-5445-2530-3   *Paperback*
       978-1-5445-2532-7   *Ebook*

In loving memory of Doris Silver Kahn

"Don't tell me
truth hurts, little girl.
'Cause it hurts like hell."

—David Bowie, "Underground"

INCLUSIVITY

I am a cisgender, straight, white woman who was raised in Ashkenazi Jewish culture. This book was written from my perspective. Singlehood happens to everyone, from every background, of every ethnicity and identity, everywhere in the world. The single community includes everyone, and every member of it is welcome here. Throughout the book, heterosexual scenarios will be used and referenced, but they are never intended to suggest that heterosexual scenarios are the *only* ones that occur within singlehood. This book is written in acknowledgment of what single women in search of relationships with single men experience in the modern dating space but not exclusively so. When the word "woman" is used, it includes *all* who identify as women.

SAFETY

Throughout the book, I will reference the agency and choice that we have as single women over the ways we participate in the dating space. This does not, in any way, include incidents of sexual assault, rape, or any other physically and mentally unsafe situations or outcomes stemming from dating or any other situation in singlehood. This book is in no way intended to serve as or replace qualified resources for depression, anxiety, trauma, or any aspect of mental health. I am an advocate for singles seeking qualified therapeutic mental health care, and I'm a proponent of resources that make these services financially accessible to all.

RESPECT

I am very direct. In a world that doesn't hold single women in high regard, I see no logic in passive language, as it delays the road to reframing. Basically, I want you to feel better, faster, so sometimes what I say may be hard to hear. At one time, it was also hard for me to say it to myself. But I did, and I learned, and now I'm sharing that knowledge with you. At no time am I presenting my work in an accusatory or demeaning tone. Everything that is said in this book is said with the utmost love and respect for single women—and comes from a woman who has lived every aspect of singlehood that is within her perspective. My work is presented here in the hope that it will lead to single women feeling better, as well as to much more respect for single women and their experiences in the future.

Contents

Introduction

We don't have to hate this. We don't have to hate being single. Has anyone ever told you that's allowed? Being single doesn't have to be a thing we fear, despise, or have shame about. It's possible to love this single life, to arrive at a place in your mind and heart where you value it so much that you refuse to give it up for anyone unworthy of you. I know it's scary to think about loving being single, because of the negative repercussions we've been led to believe come with it. The good news is, they're all nonsense. The negative narratives and limiting thoughts we have around singlehood can be rewritten, and you're already reading the book that's going to help you.

Don't be afraid to love being single. It doesn't mean you'll be single forever.

You know what being unhappily single feels like: the wanting, the searching, the dismissal, the rejection, the confusion, the exhaustion, the unfairness, the loneliness, the shame, the longing, the jealousy, the sadness, the nothing. The misery of being single—and the knowledge that it will all go away, and everything will be better, when you find a partner. And then you can't find a partner. No matter what you try, for how long you try it, you can't find someone. For months, years, or decades. I guess the most helpful thing for me to say from the start is that you're not alone.

I'm Shani Silver, I'm thirty-nine years old, and I've been single for thirteen years. I'm going to teach you how to not wince at that. I've been writing, podcasting, and building a community of single women for a long time. I'm in this world, and I know how it feels. I know how low being single can bring us, and what it's like to be willing to do *anything* to escape the shame of singlehood. I also know what it feels like when anything *still doesn't work*.

There's a way to feel better about being single that doesn't require anything other than you—just as you are. Not after you "work on yourself," or "learn to love yourself." Right *now*. For extra grins, you should also know that being single isn't actually bad. (We'll get into this in detail, but for now, just trust me.)

How do we talk about singlehood? What are the words we associate with this time in our lives? I think of *wrong*, *bad*, *flawed*, *sad*, *pathetic*, and *desperate*, for a start. That's how we've heard singlehood discussed and depicted. "Single" itself is a negative term, one so baked into our society as indicating lack that those experiencing singlehood believe there's no other way to see it. Singlehood is an *assumed* negative in need of repair via a relationship. It's so easy to casually accept society's view of singlehood and essentially never give it a second thought—or an original thought. In our society, the default state of single is *wrong*.

I hope it comforts you to know that there is most definitely another way to see singlehood, and another way to live it. I live happily single every day, while still wanting a relationship and looking forward to one. At the same time, I also don't feel so compelled to find a relationship that I make myself miserable with the search. It is possible to breathe, to let go, and to relax. If you're ready to stop being unhappy just because you're single, you're reading the right book.

This will all sound new, different, and maybe uncomfortable at first. It's okay if it takes time and practice to change the way you think and feel about being single. This doesn't have to be an instant, overnight thing. Whatever pace you're on is perfect. It took me a decade, trust me—you're already doing great.

I'm not going to tell you my dating and singlehood horror stories, because you've already heard them. You've already lived them. They're not entertainment. They're not dinner party conversation. They're tiny traumas that add up over time, and we don't deserve them. We have *so much more* to talk about than the terrible things that happen in the dating world, but for some reason, singles as a community never really talk about anything other than dating. So I'm in a bit of a rush to get started.

Imagine the deepest, darkest pit of singlehood despair, and then imagine living there for a decade. That was me. When I say I understand, when I say I sincerely needed to hear everything I'm about to tell you, please believe that I've been *through it*—because I believe you.

If you're a single woman of any age, but especially over thirty, on one side, there's societal single shaming, and on the other, there's an exhausting, belittling, and punishing dating culture. Single women are stuck in the middle. That is, quite frankly, fucked up.

Single women are not less. We are not lower status or class. We have the same value as any human being currently coupled. But the world tells us something different, every day, so we feel low. We come to understand that the only way out of singlehood unhappiness is finding a partner. But what if it's not?

For ten years, I hated every waking moment of my single, swiping life, until it exhausted me to the cliff's edge of madness. Instead of losing it, I decided to change my mind. I decided to find a way out of single misery that didn't involve finding a boyfriend. I found it, and I'm bringing single women with me, because swiping isn't working for us—but this is.

This book is designed to set us free from societal single shaming on one side and an impossible dating culture on the other, without needing a partner first. This is not a beach read; it's a guidebook. (Though feel free to read it on the beach or any other place you enjoy your free time. Oooh, that's one of my *favorite* things about singlehood: free time.)

A Single Serving Podcast, my podcast, launched in April 2019 because I wanted more content created for single women that was *not about dating*, and I couldn't find it. Everything was about the horror stories, the dating advice, the fucking *B*chelor*—everything came at singlehood as if it were a negative state of being that required dating and partnership in order to correct it. I believed there was much more to talk about, and much more respect due to single women, so I try to give us that once a week. If you'd like further support after reading this book, check it out.

Removing the shame and stigma of singlehood for yourself is thoroughly life-changing. When we love our single lives, we stop exhausting ourselves by treating every waking moment as an opportunity to find a relationship. We stop staying in relationships that aren't working, because singlehood is no longer something that sounds worse. We stop feeling crushed when a "match" or a first date doesn't turn into more, because we're not hanging every hope we have on them. We don't force ourselves to have feelings for people we feel nothing for, because we don't have to. We set ourselves free in countless ways, and we begin to live a life unburdened by the negative narratives of singlehood.

I'm often asked for my "lightbulb moment," the second I knew I wanted to change the way I thought and felt about being single, as if a switch flipped and suddenly everything changed. In reality, it wasn't just one moment—it was a series of moments that took time to come together into a completely changed way of looking at single life. You'll read about a few of them in a little while. For now, if you want to know the first time I *ever* considered that feeling better was possible, imagine this:

I was visiting home in Fort Worth, Texas, sitting in the backseat of my mother's SUV. We were running pre-Thanksgiving errands. There's nothing like sitting in the backseat as a thirty-something to spark contemplation of your entire life. At that point, I'd been dating to zero avail for six or seven years at least, and I was in a pretty low place mentally and emotionally. Squished in between the dry cleaning and the bulk artichoke dip from Costco, a thought rose up in my brain like a weather balloon.

"You don't have to find someone for your life to start."

There it was: permission. Permission to live fully, to live real. I'd never had that before. Until that moment, I never thought I was a valid adult, because I was single, and therefore missing a key component of adulthood—a relationship. It would take several more years and several more lightbulbs, but I got there. I changed my perspective, and I found a life I love without having to find someone else first. Hopefully by gathering it all in one place, I'll have made things a little more streamlined for you.

I wrote this book for all single women who are *so damned sick* of feeling ashamed, helpless, and exhausted all at the same time. We deserve wonderful relationships, and we don't deserve to be miserable until we find them.

Through single shaming, social (media) comparison, and a dating culture akin to a festering bog of chemical waste, single women receive nothing but messages telling us that we're wrong. Every product, television show, movie, song, or piece of content created for us relates to solving singlehood via dating and partnership. It's society's way of reiterating to us, over and over again, that we're not real yet.

Our dating culture and single-shaming society both tell us that our singlehood is a problem that's all our fault, while passively watching dating itself get continually more trash and honestly, a revolution is the very least we can do.

Blame isn't working for single women. All of the "this is why I'm single" memes aren't helping anyone, and honestly, they weren't funny to begin with. I don't like limiting my beliefs about singlehood and dating so much that they can be attributed to or "blamed" on anything, and certainly not solely on single women, who bear the brunt of what dating culture has become. Modern singlehood can be a miserable experience, and a lot went into crafting this culture. My personal theory (just one of them—I have many) is that dating advanced from a technological and cultural standpoint *much faster* than societal views of single women did. The words used to describe us are relics of a very outdated way of thinking about being single. We're dating in the present and being shamed in the past. Seems fair.

My fear is not that single women will "end up alone." I've yet to see a clear indication of when "end up" actually starts. Instead, my fear is that single women will continue to focus so narrowly on "finding someone" that they restrict the aperture of their lives down to a pinhole. We are sitting on the freest, most potential-filled parts of our lives. Let's reframe the way we think, and therefore feel, about being single. Let's learn how to let more light in—and live.

This is not about data and numbers. This is not yet another tool to scare single women by feeding us stats about how many more women than men attend college or whatever else people want to turn into clickbait today—while at the same time not giving us any sort of coping strategy or solution. I can't solve the numbers, but I can help you feel better no matter what they are.

This is about the day-to-day reality that affects the lives of single women and their self-worth, and how to feel better as we move through the world. Understand that you *deserve* to feel better about your singlehood, and feeling better is within your capability. There is value in you, just as you are right now. I'm sorry that societal single shaming and a dismissive dating culture have tried to cloud that value from your vision.

I will not simply point out a problem. I will provide an actual solution that's achievable, without reliance on anyone or anything outside of ourselves. Dating sucks? No shit. Let's stop sending screenshots to our friends and posting rants on social media and start actually fucking doing something about it. As mentioned, I'm quite direct. I hope you're on board.

A Single Revolution will offer more support, comfort, and strategy than an Instagram meme where the joke is made at our expense. More than a dating show that treats singles like modern-day gladiators. More than a "dating coach" who wants to take your money but still can't tell you when and where to meet your fucking husband. In order to help single women open up to new narratives, we need to reframe everything we've been groomed to believe about single life. It would also help if the book outlining that reframing wasn't embarrassing for single women to hold on public transportation. That's why this book's title and cover reflect the fact that we don't need another piece of work that assumes we are inherently "less than," self-deprecating, or in need of repair. You are not less because you're single; you are infinite because you are.

The way out of single shame involves self-worth and acknowledging a valid life full of freedom and possibility, instead of shrinking our desires and self-esteem down to crumbs because the world tells us we're lesser beings. The world is either lying or moronic, and I have no patience for single shaming either way. We have agency over what we do and how we feel, and we don't have to do or feel as we're told. We can choose to stop lowering our standards, and instead require that the rest of the world simply rise.

This book is a shame-eradicating feel-better guide for every single woman who's sick of this shit. I know how to change your perspective on being single, how to shed the shame, and how to see the real value of singlehood, rather than holding on to how flawed and in need of "fixing" the world wants us to believe we are. I know how to feel better—to feel really good—about your single life every day, and I love this community too much to keep it to myself.

We as singles can debunk the bullshit, reframe the reality, and see the value in our singlehood before it's gone. That is possible, and that is allowed.

You don't have to exhaust yourself and your sanity trying to find a relationship. You don't have to wait for a partner for your life to start. You don't have to stop wanting a relationship to start loving your single life. And you don't need a "match" to burn the negative narratives of being single right down to the ground.

Welcome to *A Single Revolution*.

The Wrongness

You're not wrong. Being single is not wrong. It's important for single women to hear that, if for no other reason than a nice change of pace. In this moment, you are living and breathing and you're worthy of existing, exactly as you are. You don't need to fix anything about yourself before you're allowed to be worthy of love from another person or from yourself. You don't need the world to forgive you for being single in order to have permission to move forward with your life. Heavy shit to start with, no? I figured we'd take care of it right up front.

The most fundamental part of reframing the way we think about our own singlehood can also be the most challenging. There is nothing wrong with you, and you are not doing anything wrong—but more than anything, *you* are not wrong. It's hard to believe these truths because we've never believed them before. We may never have even *heard* them before. But the archaic beliefs around singlehood— the assumed wrongness—have to be challenged, because they're making us feel bad. We don't deserve to feel bad simply because we haven't found partners yet in a world where, for many of us, finding partnership is *hard*.

It's time for the very notion that singlehood is a wrong state of existence, reparable only through partnership—no matter what women must endure to get there—to face its music. I can't let it get away with this anymore. The idea that "being single is wrong" isn't true just because society needs someone to shame. We're not kids in a schoolyard; we're grown adults, and I don't need the popular girls to like me anymore. The only actual consequences for being single have been invented by a) a culture that's more comfortable with partnership because it's viewed as "settled down" and you can glean *alllll* the patriarchal messages you want from that, and b) a social media space full of people who don't feel fully good about their lives unless other people are watching. Yeah, I said it.

I'm calling the wrongness on its shit. I can see what's happening to single women, because I'm one of us, and I can't sit silently while we absorb the societal shame of singlehood on one side and a punishing dating culture on the other. This isn't me being brave—this is me being fed the fuck up.

For ten actual years, I made certain assumptions about being single, because I didn't know I could think about being single any other way. I assumed that being single was a wrong state, that being in a relationship was a right state, and that until I was in a relationship, it was my responsibility to try to find someone. For a long time, my efforts were passive and casual, no different from any other chore. I approached dating apps and the pursuit of partnership in much the same way I did dishes or laundry. I was single, so I searched for someone. That's just what you *do*.

I suppose if you meet someone at some point in your search for partnership, a need for a new perspective never really presents itself. But after ten full years of online and IRL dating without even one relationship resulting, my mental shit hit the theoretical fan. I mean honestly, can you imagine doing *anything* for ten years and never accomplishing the goal? Imagine looking for an apartment for ten years and never finding one. That was me and the pursuit of partnership. No matter what I did, what I tried, or who I listened to, I never, *ever* found what I was looking for. I just found a lot of dismissiveness and mistreatment instead. But I thought that's what you do. I thought you suffer through the grind, and then the Universe rewards you with a partner. I thought this for a fucking decade.

For some reason, our clearest messages and memories always occur in the shower. Like what is it about overpriced shampoo from Sephora that sparks epiphany? I remember the very lowest point of my singlehood. My self-worth was nonexistent, my career was a source of great cruelty, and my mental health was in ribbons. One night, while I wiped stinging soap bubbles out of my contact lenses, a thought entered my head and never left: *there's a reason for this.*

In a way, the amount of dating culture horror I'd been subjected to over a decade was comical. If I didn't find it funny, I was scared of what I'd think instead. I'd swiped through, messaged, and gone out with so many men it was wondrous that I hadn't had a relationship with someone by *accident* at any point. But I never did—it was just one rejection or disappointment after another. A deep, endless void of nonmatches, ignored messages, and dates that were about as enticing as wet bread. For ten...entire...years.

It couldn't be happening to me for nothing. It wouldn't be happening just to be funny, or even to be cruel. If we're operating on a punishment model, I'd paid for any sins I'd committed or would *ever* commit five times over at that point. It made no sense, so I think my mind found some logic at the very bottom of my mental barrel. I think that's all that was left. I don't exist just to suffer through miserable dating experiences and deep singlehood shame for years on end. It was illogical to think that *that* was the only intent of my actual human life. Really? My soul came here for *this*? There had to be something else, a reason for everything I was going through. You're reading a very big reason right now.

Over time, the acknowledgment that there must be a reason grew into a bigger idea. For single people, including me, there is a way out of misery and shame that doesn't involve finding a partner first. We weren't put on Earth to wait for partnership to save us from the shame society invented. There is a way to live a genuinely happy, full, and valid single life—not a life that's "good enough" for a single girl, but one that's just as good as we've been trained to believe is waiting for us in partnership. We can have just as much happiness and validity as anyone in a couple. We start by getting rid of the wrongness.

Being single isn't a wrong way to be. This is a very basic and essential concept that single women need to understand, because its inverse is the very thing that keeps us hating our singlehood and repeating behaviors that contribute to our own misery. I don't blame us for feeling wrong; it's the only way society has ever told us single women are allowed to feel. Everything created for or about single women pertains to dating, love, sex, and finding partnership, and literally nothing else.

Dating app, after dating app, after dating app, after dating app. Dating show, after competitive dating show, after instant-marriage show where someone gets hitched to an actual stranger, and so on. Honestly, whoever greenlights these things needs a good kick in the teeth.

Charming coffee mugs and wine glasses attempt to turn solitude into quips and jokes, suggesting that "you're not drinking alone if the cat is home." As if being alone, drinking wine alone, or owning a cat are even remotely sad truths. Really? Is that all they've got to make fun of us with? *Good things?* Sounds like lazy writing to me.

The world spins singlehood as sad and wrong in any number of ways, and if it ever does spin being single as right, it paints singlehood as a permanent choice that a woman has to make, drawing a line in the sand and firmly declaring herself as someone who has "sworn off dating" to be "single by choice." That's the only way singlehood is depicted with even a shred of positivity, when you essentially commit yourself to it instead of a partner.

But what if that's not what you want? What if you want a relationship but don't think you should be unhappy until you find one? Who said single women have to choose either misery or permanence? It's possible, and allowed, to love your singlehood and want a relationship at the same time. I live that way every day.

If everything in our culture ever made for single women pertains to dating and finding love, then seriously, what are we supposed to think about our singlehood? If the focal point of all conversations about single women is "finding someone," what does that tell us about what the world thinks matters most? What does that say about what *should* matter most to us?

These messages also appear passively in the ways single women are portrayed. Think about the stories we tell about single women and the ways we've been raised in society to think about ourselves, as reflected back to us by how television, movies, songs, and endless artforms choose to style us. We're either the sad and desperate single, the hot mess, the pathetic friend, or the crazy old lady. The only happy endings we're allowed involve partnership. Even *female superheroes* have love interests (that they never get to keep, for some reason). There is a societal aversion to telling stories about happy single women who are doing great in life. The message single women receive in return is this: *Single is wrong. Fix your singleness by finding a partner, or else you're wrong.*

What about the ways coupled people are celebrated? What messages do those celebratory effusements communicate to single women? Notice the reaction when a single woman tells her family she just bought her first house, and then the reaction when her sister tells them she just got engaged. What's the more exciting news, in the family's eyes? Why is something a person worked for less worthy of celebrating than something a person found? We take each other out to dinner to celebrate new jobs with guaranteed salaries and benefits, but we throw multi-thousand-dollar weddings that ignore the statistical likelihood of a lasting marriage based on the current global divorce rate. Things that happen to single people aren't inherently less important than things that happen to people in couples, but the way we celebrate them is completely unbalanced. I'm just saying.

I know there's no celebration in singlehood. None that comes from outside of ourselves, anyway. Even when we accomplish things, there's always a film on top of it, like it needs a good Windexing. It's the notion that our accomplishments don't mean as much because we don't have "someone to share them with." Everything couples get to experience is communicated to us as good and precious. Singles, on the other hand, are digging through a digital dumpster, looking for the thing coupled people have that lets their life accomplishments finally matter.

The difficulty gets deeper, doesn't it? It gets more direct. And it often comes from people we love.

"How are you single? Are you dating? How are you dating? I bet you haven't tried this yet. Try this! This will fix your singleness. How have you not found someone yet? I can't believe you're still single."

What in the toasty hell are we supposed to do with these questions and suggestions? These constant micro-intrusions into our personal lives? I think they're actually less about someone trying to help us and more about someone trying to feel help*ful*. Do they really care? How can our singlehood possibly affect others so much that it's always their first question when we sit down to dinner? Our singlehood doesn't actually affect anyone else *at all*. They're just approaching it as if it's a wrong state, because that's what they've been taught, too. Can you imagine the reverse?

"How are you married? How happy is your marriage? Have you tried therapy? Try this kind of therapy, it will fix your unhappy marriage. I can't believe someone married you."

We never say such things to married people, because we've been taught that couplehood is sacred, protected, and right. Singlehood is appropriate for invasive small talk, but couplehood is none of our business. It's a completely illogical imbalance of respect. You don't become more worthy of respect simply because you're in a couple. You're not suddenly more human or more adult, but society doesn't understand that yet. A huge benefit in changing the way we think and feel about our own singlehood is that we stop letting society get away with this garbage.

These messages take root. When all we're shown is how prized couplehood is, and how shameful or "lesser" singlehood is, of course we're going to have a low opinion of our own singlehood.

The biggest problem with the opinions of singlehood that we develop over our lifetimes is they don't belong to us. If we've never questioned where our opinions come from, we're likely to passively think being single is wrong. Entertaining the idea that single isn't actually the wrong way to be becomes a radical act. If you're miserable and consumed by the feeling you need to "find someone," there's a way out of that feeling that doesn't involve anyone else. It involves getting fucking radical.

We're taught to seek the life state where people will finally think we're "done," so we can be treated as whole, valid human beings instead of lesser sacks of sadness who should *totally go talk to that guy at the other end of the bar, he's so cute!* (Always said loud enough for the guy to hear, of course.) I know it can feel uncomfortable to go against the broadly accepted notions and opinions surrounding singlehood. But do you feel "comfortable" with the way you think about your singlehood now? It always feels weird to think and act differently from the norm, but I can tell you the feelings of validity and worthiness you'll find on the other side are worth it.

We aren't less than other people. We aren't a lower status or class than people in couples. If you've never heard anyone say this to you before, I wish I was there to give you a hug and go to lunch with you, and we could split any appetizers you want. I know it can take time to get used to new ideas, so please be patient with and kind to yourself. The fact that singlehood isn't wrong is a new thing to hear, but it has always been true.

It's easy for me to look at a single woman and say, "You're not wrong." You're not wrong for being single, you're not wrong for thinking our modern dating culture is broken, there is nothing wrong with what you're thinking or feeling, and there's nothing inherently wrong with you just because you don't have a partner yet. It's quite another thing for her to believe it.

Reframing the way we think about our own singlehood is an unlearning. It can take time to reframe our perspective, to start seeing single life for more of its truths and fewer of its fables. It's a pretty simple process really, but that doesn't mean it won't have a big impact or require practice, patience, and self-kindness. Most of what I discuss in this book is a rewriting and reframing of common singlehood narratives. Here's a really clear and direct example of what I mean:

Old thought: *I have to sleep alone.*
New thought: *I get the whole bed.*

Take one situation that's happening and choose to see it in a different way—a way that is also true. The same thing is happening in both scenarios, but how we choose to view it is different. Choose to change your perspective. All this swiping has narrowed our vision down to an opening the size of a wet paper straw, and as a result, I believe we're missing out on so much of what's actually happening.

Single women deserve an upgrade. We deserve to feel better about being single, and we deserve to love every single day of our lives. To break out of hating something you've tried to "fix" for years and can't, reframe the way you think about it. With practice, we can change our thoughts and feelings around our own singlehood, so we learn not only to stop hating it but also to start seeing its value. It's hard to hate something when you can see how it's doing you good.

With practice, we can have a higher opinion of singlehood than society ever gave us permission to, and we can live more fully, with more self-worth.

Has anyone ever told you that you're just...*allowed* to be single? Has that message ever been communicated to you? Even if it hasn't, it's still true. You're allowed to exist as a single person because *that's what you're doing right now.* Singlehood is a valid state of being, and there's no rule, law, or reality that makes a single person inherently lesser in status or value than someone with two names on their mail.

Singlehood is a valid state. I could argue that it's the more natural one. We were born and exist as individuals, so how could *continuing to be an individual* be bad? I am a whole, valid person who is not unfinished without a romantic attachment to someone else. It's a ring, not a vital organ, you guys.

Sometimes, I actually worry about people who don't see themselves as whole without their partner. I play that tape through to the end, and I'm afraid for anyone who can't see wholeness and validity in themselves unless someone else claims them. That doesn't sound like much self-worth to me, and I'm afraid for anyone who hasn't found self-worth *before* partnership. I fear for these people if and when their relationships end. As singles, we have the freedom and time to establish genuine self-worth, independent of anyone else. We also have the space to see singlehood for all its positives and benefits, so that we're no longer afraid to return to singlehood if we need to.

I see my singlehood as a gift, because it's given me more than any relationship ever has. I know things now that I never bothered to learn when I was in a relationship, when I was attaching my worth to the fact that someone loved me—or afterward, when all I could do was zero in on finding someone new, swiping through faces like a maniac in every spare moment. I never took the gift of time to learn what I know now, because I was always ignoring it in favor of trying to fix my singlehood problem. I had been programmed to believe that chore was my responsibility, in order to stop being wrong.

What I know today is I am correct as I exist right now. I have proof in the fact that I've been single for thirteen years and haven't burst into flames yet. If this was wrong, I'd see proof of wrongness. Instead, I see just the opposite.

What really solidifies a reframe is seeing the good. I don't just want us to see things from a different angle, I want a *good* one. I want to take things further than just "singlehood is not wrong." I want to rewrite my beliefs even more powerfully into "singlehood is *also right*." Have you ever taken the time to ask yourself what's good and right about being single? I never did. I was too sold on society's idea of how wrong I was, so I was desperate to finally be "right" by finding a partner. But I was always right. I was always a lot of other things, too.

I'm free. I compromise with no one. I accommodate no one. My home is mine, my mess is mine, and my money is mine. My schedule only ever contains what I want or need to do. I never have to justify or explain my actions, and I never have to deal with anyone else's behavior, either. I follow my curiosities in life—I have time to. Everything in my world is tailored to my tastes, and mine alone. I discovered all this and a lot more by entertaining the idea that I didn't have to be miserable all the time just because I was a totally normal, natural thing to be—single. I am the most free I have ever been, the smartest I have ever been, and the most at peace I have ever been. You can't tell me that the opposite of those things would make me better at relationships. I mean, you can try, but I'll laugh at you. My singlehood is a gift. Yours is, too.

There is so much here. So much to this life. If all we ever know of singlehood is that it's wrong, we'll spend all our time trying to fix it, and we'll miss the good—we'll miss the opportunities that singlehood affords us. I don't want us to wait until we find someone to feel good. We're allowed to feel good right now.

I spent a decade in hell and found my way out by choosing to think about and feel my singlehood with more truth—and less failure and shame. I have experienced the very depths of the lows, and if my heart belongs to anyone, it belongs to those of us who are still down there. I want you to know there is so much good waiting for you, and you don't have to find someone else in order to experience it.

As I write this to you, I am single, and the miserable person I used to be is now no more than memory and motivation. I know it's possible to feel better about being single because I did it. If I did, you can. I know I'm right.

2

More or Less

M any years ago, when there was still a "2" in front of my age, I went on vacation with four of my dearest friends from college. It was two couples and me. I've never been the sort of gal to let a lack of consistent sex and someone to deal with spiders for me keep me away from time with friends or a few days on a beach, so I was super excited to go.

When we got to our vacation rental, we did the inevitable politeness dance in which the couple who did the most planning work for the trip got the master bedroom, the other couple got the room with the double bed and the exercise bike, and I got the glorified closet containing a set of bunk beds and a shelf with the extra towels. Every night that I spent on that plank of a bed, staring up at the underside of the bunk above me, the seeds of my current career took root.

I was no less a grown adult than everyone else in that house, but it was implied that I'd get the shittiest sleeping situation, because I was single. It was a bunk bed, there was room for two—but it went to me, because I'm "just" one person.

Why the hell do couples get better *everything* than single people? What about a couple makes their comfort and togetherness so inherently sacred that we *assume* the single person gets the lesser side of things?

You've slept on the couch in a vacation rental. You've sat at the kids' table. You've taken whatever seat is left over at dinner after the couples all sit down next to each other first. But have you ever asked yourself why? Or have you just gone along with society's (low) opinion of single people and adopted it as your own? It's been at least ten years since that trip, and I'm still angry I didn't ask one of the couples to take the bunk-bed room for a night. (For the record, I'm sure they would have, but I was *completely* unable to reframe my own mindset around singlehood back then.)

It's never blatant; there aren't signs in restaurants directing single people to sit at the bar (though you totally should anyway—it's my favorite place to sit). It's implied and assumed. Have you ever moved on an airplane so that a couple could sit together, as if the distance in the sky between Chicago and Newark were simply too great a time span for them to be out of arm's reach? One time I refused, because the seat I would have had to take was the one next to the bathroom. I felt guilty about that for years, but I don't anymore. If you want seats together, buy them, or take a different flight. Just because you signed up to be in a couple doesn't mean I have to sign up to put you first.

We never put couples out, only singles. What kills me about this is the *implied* status assigned to singles and couples. Couples, by virtue of the fact that they've decided to be a couple, are viewed in society as better, more worthy, or on a higher life level than single people. Couples come first, get prioritized and upgraded, and receive special treatment in countless aspects of life, when essentially all they've done is decided to stop doing something that's annoying anyway (dating) and split one-bedroom rent.

Why do we as singles participate in the assumption that couples are human beings of elevated status? I can't do that anymore. If my refusal to place other people above myself in importance is jarring to couples in my life, I'm quite comfortable reminding them of all the times I, as a single person, was jarred by everything I wasn't entitled to because my left ring finger was bare. (Also, we can stop saving this finger. Wear any rings on it that you want. It's an entire finger that belongs to you—you don't have to ignore it and leave it blank when it's perfectly capable of holding jewelry.)

Is refusing to prioritize couples selfish? Or is it just living through a single adulthood while each prioritization of couples adds up over time and finally boils the pot over? There is nothing about two people in a couple that is inherently more special, more accomplished, more worthy, or more deserving of special treatment in society than me. We are all just people. The jig is *up*.

Okay, so...weddings. While I'll spare us all a deep dive into how ridiculously overblown in terms of price and expectation these simple ceremonies have become, what I won't gloss over is the message that the importance of weddings communicates to single people, over and over again. We've made the most significant, "best" days of our lives belong to those who have found something outside of themselves to bind to, but we rarely celebrate the things single people have accomplished all on our own with any real fervor. What do you think that imbalance tells single people about how important and valued we are in society?

"No, no, single person. You don't get a party—not until you're more than yourself and are two people. Until then, go sit over there with all the other singles who made our seating arrangements have too many odd numbers."

When you don't have an automatic person to sit next to, it's assumed you'll "be fine" sitting anywhere. If you've ever spent money on plane tickets, meals, hotel rooms, and transportation for a friend's wedding only to be seated at a table with all the other odds and ends instead of getting a seat next to the friends in couples you *actually* know from law school, you know that sitting anywhere is actually pretty insulting. I'm tired of waiting for the main course to be served so that I can drag a chair over to where my friends are; I don't know about you.

The implied contract that people will spend any amount of money, attend any number of events, and still not get a fucking plus-one so they don't have to make small talk with someone's new husband's cousin all night is done. The entitlement is done. The implied financial burdens are done. We are allowed, as valid single people, to normalize saying no to celebrating other people's couplehood. Not just when it costs too much, but when it costs anything. Wedding culture has become a disgusting pageant of self-importance and entitlement, and you're allowed to stop participating right this minute. If the friend "never speaks to you again," maybe that's for the best.

It's so childish, still clinging to societal markers of validity like couplehood and marriage. We give so much respect and privacy to what happens "behind closed doors," but we don't celebrate human beings on an exalted level unless we have a damn good idea of what's going on in there.

"Omg, you guys are having SEX? With only each other? Forever?! LET'S PARTY."

In the wider world that makes couples feel like they're worth more than singles, these observations will sound like some pretty petty shit. Having a problem with celebrating couples or weddings always earns the single woman the markers of bitterness or jealousy. That's because those judgments are coming from outside the single woman, while inside, the single woman is just exhausted with being made to feel like she matters less than two people who have consistent consensual sex and someone to try new restaurants with. There are enough perks to couplehood without insulating them from me telling the goddamned truth.

And anyway, I'm not speaking to the coupled world right now. I'm speaking to the single world, to the woman reading this on a park bench, or on her couch, or while waiting to board a plane. I'm speaking to the world that never feels celebrated, while watching people who already got something awesome (partnership) receive *more* awesome things like societal acceptance, praise, celebration, and gifts, while all we get is, "So, are you *seeeeing anybodyyyyy?*" every goddamned time we sit down to brunch.

If couplehood is that incredible, isn't *that* the thing they get? Why do we also have to pool *our* money to sponsor every component of their honeymoon? Your tax advantages, shared bills, consistent company, physical touch, and knowledge that if shit hits the fan you're not alone to deal with it *are* your gifts, Susan. I'm not also buying you a fucking air fryer.

If you want to have a wedding someday, have a wedding. Just have it because it's meaningful to the partnership, not because you think it finally makes you a valid adult. You were never less valid than people in couples, and I'm sorry the world has ever groomed us to feel any other way. But believe me, if you still hold on to feelings of lessness, I get it. I felt less than, too, for about a decade. Of course, I did. I was living in a world that told me, at every opportunity, just how much less valid and less worthy of respect my singlehood and I were.

Our privacy as single people is less sacred. Our sex as single people, because it's often with ourselves, is less valid as sex at all. The marital relationship—with all its highs, lows, and epic fights—is considered too important and private a thing to inquire about or intrude on. But sit down to dinner with a pile of friends, and the first thing they do is: *Go on any good dates lately? How's dating going? I love hearing your horror stories!*

The next time a married person asks me to tell them a dating horror story, I will agree, but only if they agree to tell me the story of the last time they thought about leaving their partner. Because my romantic life isn't entertainment any more than theirs is, and I don't know any other way to teach the non-single world that particular lesson.

"How's dating going?" is a particularly tough one for me, because when it's asked with consistency and priority, it implies to singles that dating is their center. It implies that dating is *the* thing going on with them. How's dating going? I don't know, Stacy—how happy is your marriage? Because if you're married, I'll just assume it's your responsibility to work on making it a happy one. That's what I've decided is *your* center. I've also decided it's my business, so let's order a sauvignon blanc, and you can tell me all about it.

I really don't want to reference *The B*chelor* any more than necessary, but now seems like a good time to make this point: single people are not modern-day gladiators or entertainment of any kind. We don't exist to give people something to tweet and cringe about while they sit on the couch eating dinner. Because while single people "looking for love" might be entertaining to those who already have it, or those who aren't the ones being filmed, someone had to live through that "looking for love" experience. While they did, millions of people were watching, no matter how it felt.

The search for love and companionship has long been utilized for public entertainment. *The Dating Game* and *Singled Out* come to mind. But *The B*chelor* is an entire franchise inspired by a pile of taffeta-clad women fighting over a bouquet, and it makes me sick to my stomach.

Single people as entertainment hurts me. It hurts me because as human beings, when someone gives us entertainment, we tend to be entertained. We tend not to ask ourselves if what we're watching is really okay. Colosseums of people used to applaud the death of the defeated gladiator—his actual death. The life of a gladiator didn't matter much; what mattered was the entertainment of the people. Thankfully, we've moved past watching death for fun and are now content with entertainment where the blood is made of corn syrup (although we're still obsessed with true crime). We've moved on to gladiators of another kind, the single kind, and I'm hurt when I see that it's now the hearts, dignity, and desires of single people that don't matter much. We are entertainment for everyone else.

Can you name a competition-style show where we watch a group of people live through really tough times in their marriages and try to avoid divorce? There aren't shows full of couples trying to have a baby, first one to conceive and make it to twelve weeks wins a hundred grand—such a program will never exist, nor should it. The intimacies of couples are considered sacred, but the intimacies of single people are available without commercials if you pay a little extra. All the while, the very existence of "competition" shows where people "find love" at the end suggests to singles that their singlehood is *so wrong* that if necessary, they should stoop to the level of letting the world watch them compete to end it. Can you think of one date in your entire history that you'd want a national audience for?

I don't ask myself why participants in single-shaming reality shows signed up. I know their reasons: they want to get famous, they want to be actors, they want to be able to charge more on Cameo, and maybe some of them actually believe that their participation can lead to love. That's all fine for them, but the continued existence of these shows reiterates to everyone watching—including single people ourselves—that being single is less, and that "fixing" our singlehood with partnership is something worth "winning" at any cost.

I'm always surprised by how many human beings flock to their screens to watch other human beings flay themselves. Maybe I have too much empathy, but I can't watch the humiliation of others and call it entertainment. It makes me feel physically ill. I think people who make this kind of TV are bullies who couldn't give less of a shit about the feelings and mental well-being of participants. I have been bullied, so I know bullying when I see it, and I also know how it feels. Singlehood-centered reality television is bullying, just with better hair and makeup.

We live in a society that prioritizes and rewards couples, while demeaning and punishing singles. The message is if you're single, you matter less than couples, couples are better than you, you are beneath them. The world reiterates these messages to us in all the ways I've already mentioned, and countless others.

Except it's all bullshit. It isn't actually the truth—it's just what society has decided to go along with. The sooner you stop participating, the sooner you can feel just as valid, worthy, and "more" as anyone with two names on a lease. It might feel a little uncomfortable at first, but how comfortable was I in that bunk bed? Here's a quick reframe:

Old thought: *Oh, they're in a couple. They're better than me, because they accomplished couplehood. I'm not as good as they are.*

New thought: *Finding partnership is not an accomplishment deserving of preferential treatment. Couples aren't more important or deserving than I am. We are all the exact same amount of human, and I don't have to prioritize people just because they're partnered.*

Single people are not lesser people than those in couples, and when we acknowledge that fact, maybe we'll start asking society to treat us as such. Maybe it's an email to the group before the trip that lets everyone know you'll need a room with a door and a (real) bed. Anything else isn't a house big enough for your group, because sleeping on the couch isn't your job so that everyone else's vacation can be cheaper. If they complain, remind them how much your plane ticket to their wedding cost you.

Maybe it's letting the bride and groom know that you don't need a plus-one, but you'd really appreciate being seated with people you know. If that feels like an imposition or too much to ask, are you really good enough friends with these people to attend their wedding? Especially if it's out of town?

Sit in the plane seat you selected and paid for. I'm sorry if the couple that didn't book far enough in advance or missed a flight has to suffer the agony of physical distance for a few hours. (The one exception I make is when parents and kids need to sit together—I'm not a monster. Okay, I am: I only move to get myself the hell away from the kids.) If anyone complains, gently let them know that being apart for a few hours is actually nothing compared to the time you've spent apart from your future lover. I'm on thirteen years; what about you?

When you arrive at the restaurant, sit the fuck down. Don't awkwardly wait or confirm where the couples would like to sit before you feel welcome enough to join the table. Sit where you like, and if that separates a couple, suggest you all play by *Downton Abbey* rules tonight and no one sits next to their partner. Honestly, if you're dining with people who see you as a threat to their couplehood just by *sitting next to their spouse* for the length of an appetizer and entrée, you do not need to hang out with them again. I'm not trying to charm your husband away from you, Margaret—we're talking about how the quality of Hulu Originals programming has increased of late.

You are not less. You are just as much, and just as worthy, as everyone else currently coupled. Your singlehood is not a negative about you—it's simply a fact about you. Anyone who sees your singlehood as a negative is the one who is lacking perspective, as opposed to you lacking a partner.

We let our presumed lack place us in life's little backseat. It's harmful to live your own life in a way that reinforces the misconception that you matter less than couples. Beyond harmful, it's limiting. I wonder what single people are missing out on because we're letting couples cut in front of us in terms of who gets to be real and who doesn't.

When it comes to societal opinions of singlehood and couplehood, we lack balance. I think it's human nature to look at two things and assign "good" to one and "bad" to the other. Humans are the fucking worst! It isn't about couplehood being better than singlehood *or* singlehood being better than couplehood. It's about the two versions of life being equal in value, and equal in status. No law says we can't find a balance (except, of course, for tax codes and many other regulations, and if you're curious about those, I strongly suggest you look into the work of Dr. Bella DePaulo).

There is no reason why single people, particularly single women, cannot be seen and treated on the same life level, with the same amount of reverence and respect, that we give to people in couples. Again, it's a marriage license, not a royal title—everybody calm down.

There's so much that's special about you as a single person, because you are a *person*. I'm sorry that the world doesn't support the celebration of our specialness until we have "someone to share it with." If something good happens to you and you don't feel anything because you don't have anyone to "share it with," I am so deeply sorry. But I also know why you'd feel that way. Society teaches us that having someone to share things with is what matters more than literally all the other things.

So how do we fix it? How do we find our validity and moreness in a world that only wants to celebrate two people who can stop using condoms? As so often happens within the single community, we have to throw our own party.

How do you want to be celebrated? What would you like to celebrate? Has anyone ever told you that you don't need to wait for someone to throw you a shindig? (I love the word shindig.) There is nothing about singlehood that holds you back from living life just as fully and with just as much validity as couples. It's everything we've *chosen to accept* about society's opinion of singlehood that holds us back. We can choose to stop accepting that we're "less than" couples—and start living and participating in more of life.

Another thing that's really key to understanding singlehood, and the ways we choose to celebrate it, is our celebrations and accomplishments are not consolation prize versions of those things. The blowout bash you throw yourself for your fortieth birthday isn't a stand-in for a wedding. You're allowed to go apeshit on a birthday and then later *have a wedding, too.* The private dining room you rent to celebrate becoming a partner in your firm isn't "sad" because you did it for yourself. The dinner party you throw at your place after you successfully defend your thesis isn't "good enough for a single person." There isn't anything less about these celebrations simply because you are single—unless you believe there is.

So much of feeling better about being single—and feeling like you can live a full, valid, *happy* life this way—comes down to choice. Singlehood doesn't actually have any rules to it apart from the rules we impose upon ourselves. When we stop settling for the version of singlehood that society has fed to us through its messaging and shed the shame of lessness that the tired-ass narratives of singlehood want us to feel, there's actually an incredible life waiting. I worry when we accept ourselves as less in life status and validity than couples, we're missing it. We're missing an incredible life.

Ask anyone what their favorite part of singlehood is, and they'll say *freedom*. The freedom to do what you want, when you want, how you want, where you want, literally 100 percent of the time. Compromise is amazing, and while I look forward to doing lots of healthy, productive compromising in my future relationships, right now...fuck that shit. You don't have to compromise with anyone! Everything is exactly as you like it, tailored to you, for the entirety of your singlehood. If all you can focus on is how not having a partner means you're not real yet, you're wasting precious freedom and choice. I don't want you to waste it, because it's really, really fun.

This is all about rewriting old, negative, *lying* narratives around singlehood, and the entire time you've been reading this chapter, I know at least one of them has been in the back of your mind. I know about the fear of choosing to be happily single. The fear is an old narrative that tells us, in the privacy of our minds somewhere, that if we start being happily single, that's the same thing as choosing to be single forever. If you've been hearing that in your head, now or ever, the next chapter is for you.

3

Single Is Not a Vengeful God

L isten, self-forgiveness will be a running theme throughout this book, because it will serve you very well as you reframe singlehood. What I'm going to discuss in this chapter has a tendency to make single women feel bad or at fault, and that is *not* my goal. There's enough shame out there for us in society without me giving you more. My intent is not to cause further strife, but instead to promote reframing and healing. Forgive yourself for ever believing *any* of the bullshit narratives around singlehood, because of *course* we believed them. We were literally never told anything else. It's hard to prefer perspectives you've never heard before.

One of my favorite, and by favorite of course I mean *least* favorite, narratives around singlehood is that we're not allowed to like it. We have to hate our singlehood and want it to end as soon as possible. If we dare develop something even *resembling* contentment or happiness while single, we run the risk of the following:

1. Angering and confusing the relationship gods—if we don't hate this, they'll never give us a boyfriend!

2. "Coming across" as someone who doesn't need or want a relationship, thereby repelling all potential partners like some sort of dating citronella.

3. Being single longer, or forever.

Singlehood as a negative is so ingrained in us that we think if we stop hating it, we'll be punished with more of singlehood itself. Because honestly, I can't think of any other reason why a single woman would choose to stay in single misery when she can let it go and be happy instead. But there's resistance. There's resistance to seeing singlehood in a positive light, because we associate that with "giving up," "choosing singlehood," and other things we don't want to be a part of. We want to be partnered—sometimes we even think we *need* to be partnered—and the assumption is that the only way to become partnered is to toil through the difficulties and discomforts of dating and singlehood. *Enjoy singlehood? Are you crazy?! If we like it, it will never end!*

The false narrative is that loving singlehood means we will never be loved by someone else—as though our singlehood happiness somehow communicates a lack of relationship desire. And we need to be communicating relationship desire at all times, or else how will anyone ever know we want a relationship?! So we fear a mindset where singlehood isn't the worst thing ever, because, of course, we want to be loved. I really hope there is some solace for you in the fact that this is all hot garbage.

Obviously, singlehood isn't something we can be punished with, because it isn't a bad thing in the first place. It's beautifully free, full of potential, void of compromise, and we get the whole couch. But for now, believe me—I get it. I get what it feels like to think you have to avoid being happily single, or reject the idea entirely, because you're afraid that there are actual repercussions.

Pain, endless longing, desperation, and simply centering dating and searching for someone in our day-to-day lives are not prerequisites for partnership. There's a part of me that actually thinks these things *delay* the very thing we want by always focusing on it so intensely, but I digress.

Your present misery isn't required payment for future happiness. How much misery have you already invested? What has the return on that investment been? You are allowed to be happy now and also find a relationship at any time. Dating is the one area of life where effort doesn't match reward, and it never has to. You will hear me say this throughout this book because it's very true, and not often acknowledged: searching for a relationship and finding one don't actually *need to have* anything to do with each other, so you might as well enjoy your life in the meantime. We'll explore this concept more later, but think of every couple you know who met by accident, instead of because one of them was obsessed with dating and hunting down the other like a maniac.

You don't have to hate your singlehood for your singlehood to end. That's not required. People who are happily single find partnership, too. Too much of my "meantime" was miserable, because I thought it *had* to be, or I'd be single forever. Here's what will really pluck your eyebrows: maybe my meantime wasn't meantime at all—maybe it was just as valid as my future partnered time will be. I know, wild.

Let's talk about how we "come across." I am *so sick* of single women worrying about how we come across. I am tired of the constant worry about how we present ourselves to the world and the belief that until we "find someone," we have to view ourselves as fucking bait.

We do not exist as single women simply to attract single men (or single women, or single anyone). We are allowed to live more than that. When I say things like this, I understand they sound kind of basic, but I haven't heard even basic truths about singlehood ever communicated to us as a cohort of people. All I've ever heard is, "Have you tried online dating? That might work! Let me see your profile—I want to make sure you're doing it right." (And other completely unsolicited thoughts on how to end something that is immediately presumed to be a negative.)

We never tell the positive truths about being single; we only ever speak about how to end it. When people only approach something about us by presuming it's wrong, what do you think that tells us over time about what we are? So yeah, it's basic for me to tell you that you get to do more with your life than worry about how cute you look every time you leave the house because "you never know," but I want you to hear it in case you never have before. We are fielding far too many messages to the contrary, and I'm allowed to offer a little balance.

To worry about how we come across is inherently to alter it. For years, *countless* years, I lived in a state of permanently adjusting myself. I worried about what I wore, my hair, my makeup, my weight, every word out of my mouth, whether I was sweating, my body language, and so on to the point that I couldn't enjoy being out in public and I could never just *relax*, because I was so goddamned worried about whether or not I'd reel in a man that day. I used to correct my facial expressions while listening to friends speak in public because I was worried I didn't look happy enough (good ol' resting bitch face), and if I didn't look happy, a man across the room might be deterred from coming up to me and saying hello. No one ever came up to me and said hello anyway, regardless of how much I fucking smiled, but these are the things that I used to spend mental energy on. Not to mention my head was permanently on a swivel, always looking for viable options. Literally all of my plans were centered on finding someone—even if they were actually about something else, like seeing my friends. Is anyone else tired? I am *spent*.

The only thing you ever need to "come across" as is who you actually are. Your authenticity is absolutely vital. It's the very thing that both allows you to live a comfortable, happy life in your own skin, *and* it's the thing that attracts the right people for you, to you.

There's a cruel twist to the thought that we're not allowed to be happy single because we're worried that makes us seem "too independent" (whatever that means) or as not wanting partnership. How the hell being happy and thriving in our own lives can possibly communicate that we don't want to be loved by others is baffling to me. But I used to buy into that narrative. I've since forgiven myself for doing so.

Someone who is happy, comfortable in their existence, drinking in life, and fully living it could *never*, in my opinion, repel people. I believe just the opposite. I believe happiness and finding joy in being alive draws people in. But when all we choose to focus on is *find him find him find him find him find him find him*, it can be almost impossible to find joy.

The search, in our current dating culture, is not joyful. It is a grind, it is punishing, and it lets us down, over and over again. Singlehood isn't the miserable thing; dating is—and dating has been letting singlehood take the blame for its bad behavior for far too long. Dating is a *huge* cause of singlehood misery, but we just keep participating in it, because we're scared that if we let it go and entertain the idea of being happy just as we are, we'll be alone forever. Remember: forgive yourself for ever believing this shit. Of course, we believed it. We were groomed to.

There are no relationship gods that you have to make offerings of misery to in order to get married one day. That isn't real. I see so much pain in this—so much sadness and self-loathing every time someone makes a "this is why I'm single" joke that was never funny. It's a choice to stay in that low space and constantly search and date and claw at any opportunity for partnership from a place of misery. Do you think that's a productive place to date from, one where you think a relationship is going to save you? How long do you think a relationship will last when you "need" it compared to *wanting* it?

Choosing to stay miserably single because you think that's the only way the Universe is ever going to throw you a bone (pun obviously intended) is complete crap. I need you to know that loving your life and being happy right now—not *only* when you find someone—can never, ever be the thing that keeps you single longer. Singlehood happiness isn't something that deserves punishment by taking longer for you to find a partner. That just doesn't make any sense.

As single women, we have to stop thinking every action we take somehow has to be about finding someone. We've been trained to center our singleness and center the search for someone, so much so that we can forget to center ourselves. You matter more than whether or not you have something "going on" in your dating life. You matter completely independent of how much "effort" you're putting into dating. And if dating is making you unhappy, you are allowed to center yourself and your happiness instead, even if you think doing so means you'll be single longer. There is no correlation between how hard you date and how likely you are to find someone, as evidenced by how hard you've *already dated*, so you might as well stop trying so goddamned hard at something that sucks, and instead give being happily single a try.

You cannot be punished for being happy. Furthermore, singlehood is not a punishment. I know we've been taught it is. I know how scared we are to be happy single, because I know how we've been trained to believe that it makes us unattractive. Please stop. Please give yourself permission to stop clinging to singlehood misery because you think that's the only way the world will ever give you a relationship. You are allowed to leave the misery behind and meet your next partner, too.

There's another narrative that's relevant to discuss here. I've seen it come up often in the single space, and readers and listeners have brought it up in *many* emails and DMs. I know it's a pervasive and common concern among single women. It is also desperately in need of reframing. It's the idea that we can either be happy with our singlehood *or* want a relationship—never both.

We, as singles, do not have to choose either being happily single *or* wanting relationships. That is not a thing. We can be happily single *and* want a relationship at the same time. That's allowed.

I see far too many rules in the single space being imposed upon us *by* us, and we'll explore this further in a later chapter. But for now, who says you have to choose between wanting a relationship *or* being happy as a single person? Where is that rule written? Or is it just something we tell ourselves because that's what we've been taught to believe? Have we been programmed to think being happily single means we're not "doing enough" about our single-hood problem? Have we equated singlehood happiness with laziness? I think we have, and I think it's bullshit.

I see singles really struggling with this. We pair every morsel of letting go of singlehood misery with instant guilt that we're not "doing enough" or "trying hard enough" to end our singlehood. These beliefs run deep, but it is possible to reframe them and feel better. We shouldn't feel guilty for refusing to subject ourselves to more dating and more "trying" if those efforts are making us unhappy and never delivering the return we want to see. There is no guilt in being happy, but the pervasiveness of singlehood shame and lack make us believe something different.

Again, dating is one area of life where effort doesn't have to match reward. You can date for a literal decade and never even have one relationship result from that effort. That's what happened to me. I miserably, endlessly dated for ten years, thinking I had to keep going—because if I let go, if I loosened my grip on "trying," I'd be single longer. This illogical pattern totally ignored that I'd been single for a pretty fucking long time already. It was only when I let go, when I admitted to myself that I was allowed to breathe, that my whole life didn't have to revolve around dating and "finding someone," that I found the happiness I thought a relationship would bring me.

Sometimes I think happy single women scare people. I think our freedom, our joy, and our thriving can somehow come across as a negative. Instead of internalizing that negativity, I try to have empathy for someone who sees a happy single woman as a threat—because if my happiness makes you feel bad, I'm not sure your happiness exists at all. Maybe I'm a reminder of someone else's misspent years. Maybe I am the embodiment of the freedom they don't have in their relationships. Whatever the reason my confidence, satisfaction, and happiness with singlehood makes other people think poorly of me, I genuinely couldn't give less of a shit. I care far more about my singlehood joy even *potentially* inspiring other singles to pursue the same. It can be extremely difficult to stop caring about what other people think. Please know it's okay if that change takes time, small steps, and practice. It's worth it.

Understand we have no idea how "long" we will be single. We have no idea how, when, or where we will connect with our future partners. We don't know, and no one else (certainly no one else who wants to charge you money) can ever tell you. I see this as a good thing! This isn't up to us. It's up to luck, fate, chance, the Universe—whatever, but our own happiness before, during, and after meeting our partners *is* up to us. Choosing to see the value in singlehood could never, ever keep us from a moment that we do not control.

There is no way for your singlehood happiness to be a detriment to you. Any belief that it can somehow hinder you is centering dating and "finding someone" as your primary purpose—and removing *you* as your primary purpose. Here are some reframes for you:

Old thought: *I have to hate being single, or I'll always be single.*

New thought: *Dating superstitions aren't helping me find a partner any faster. If hating singlehood made a partner show up, I definitely wouldn't still be single right now. Maybe hating singlehood doesn't actually solve anything. Maybe I can give liking singlehood a try and see what happens.*

Old thought: *I don't have someone, so I have to keep searching.*

New thought: *Being single isn't a sentence. I am not required to spend my actual life in pursuit of someone else.*

Old thought: *Being single is bad.*

New thought: *Wait...what's so bad about this again?*

We can lose ourselves in the search. I know that from an overwhelming amount of experience. I am sometimes ashamed of how much of my adulthood I wasted swiping into nothingness. How much time I spent worrying about how I "came across," trying to adjust myself to make myself more appealing to men. I ignored how any adjustment I made that attracted a man would have been inauthentic and something I'd have to maintain forever. I think of how I could have spent those ten years instead, what I could have learned, how I could have grown as a person, what I could have accomplished if I'd spent that time another way. Then I remember that I spent *plenty* of years living in shame, and I don't need to give myself *more* shame by regretting not walking away from singlehood misery and the punishments of dating culture sooner.

I choose to see that time as an education. I choose to do something productive with what I learned. I let those ten years remind me of how I want to live the next ten, the next twenty. I remember the strength and lessons it took to pull myself out of a single life that I vehemently hated. I remember I did it: I made it out of there and into a place where I genuinely value and appreciate my single time. So instead of throwing my singlehood away at the first opportunity, I will be happily content in it until someone comes along who is just as wonderful as my singlehood, if not better.

In prior iterations of myself, I thought I deserved less and less of what I wanted, because I was single for longer and longer. I equated time spent single with a decrease in my value as a human being. At my lowest point, I would have accepted anyone who paid attention to me that I didn't find repulsive as a potential partner. Now, it's going to take a hell of a lot more than that. I am so deeply grateful that I was able to make this shift, and I want it for other singles, too.

It is entirely possible to love your single life and look forward to your next partnership—even pursue it to the extent you're comfortable—at the exact same time. That is reality and truth. Anything else is bullshit superstition. Falsehoods keep us small in our singleness and prevent us from appreciating the joys of single life. There is so much good available to you during your singlehood, and I want us all to see it. When we can't see the value of singlehood, we only see value in continuing to try and change it. And we continue to pursue partnership at any emotional and financial cost.

You will never be punished for letting go of singlehood misery. Your future relationships do not require you to hate being single. Your happiness is allowed to happen, right now, while simultaneously leaving you open to other kinds of happiness in the future. Living happily single can coexist with wanting your next relationship. You are allowed to have both.

4

Paying for Maybes

One of the hardest truths for me to face in my work within the singlehood space is that I can't protect everyone. I can't Batman my way around every app, every date, and every encounter that has the potential to harm or even just disappoint a single woman. That doesn't mean I don't want to—it just means I'm going to need your help.

I've yet to find a scenario that fills me with more carbonated lava than when people try to make money off of single women without ever having to deliver what they're choosing to market to us in the first place. Since I can't stop this from happening, maybe I can illuminate it for you, and you can make your own decisions about how or if you participate.

Imagine paying a barista for a cup of coffee, but they're never required to give it to you. They're not actually selling coffee; they're just selling the opportunity to be in the coffee shop. You can watch it being made and inhale its aromas, but this coffee shop never has to promise or deliver actual coffee. You might see other customers get coffee, but you never get yours. You just stand there, thinking how nice a cup of coffee would be right now—you know, the one you thought you'd get because you paid for it. Then you pay for *another* cup of coffee, thinking maybe that will do the trick, because you see some people getting coffee. You repeat this process over, and over, and *over* again...without ever getting any goddamned coffee.

That's how the dating industry treats single women. It knows what we want, it knows we'll come hang out in its space because we've been led to believe that what we want is sold there, and it knows how to bait us into paying for a chance to get what we want, forever.

We want to see dating as something other than what it has actually become. We want it to be fun, full of butterflies, an exciting part of life, and something we enjoy participating in. Instead, dating has become a difficult, often punishing, minimally rewarding task that can often feel like a second job—only instead of getting paid to do it, *you're* the one who's paying to be there.

Just because we want to see dating and "finding love" in a certain light, that doesn't mean there isn't something less wholesome happening in the dark. As single women, we need to see and understand that modern dating culture has given birth to a thriving industry, and we need to see this industry with immense clarity if we are going to be in the right frame of mind to participate. Or we need to allow this clarity to support us in walking away from the industry altogether, so that we don't feel like we're "lowering our chances." My stars, I hate that phrase.

I'm not an advocate for singlehood. I'm an advocate for single women feeling good while they're single. I'm also an advocate for permanently deleting all of your dating apps, but I won't terrify you with that just yet. You can look forward to it in a later chapter. By the time you get there, you might even be on board.

The core of why I don't like dating apps, and why I don't like the dating industry in general, is it's all based on maybes. Single people are paying for countless maybes, and because our society so severely shames single women, we're the ones the dating industry can take advantage of more than all of the single—LOL—men we're swiping through.

What do I mean? Dating apps aren't charging you for a relationship. They're charging you for the possibility of one. Matchmakers aren't charging to find your husband for you; they're charging to introduce you to a few people. Dating coaches aren't charging to tell you where, when, and how to meet your partner, even if that's the only actual information you need in order to find them. The industry is allowed to promise nothing, deliver nothing, and still continue to thrive.

You're paying for maybes. You're never paying to become coupled, which is presumably the reason you sought out the dating industry in the first place. Instead, you're paying for something that *might work*. Would you pay a gardener to plant flowers that might grow? Would you pay a personal chef for food that might be edible? Would you pay an employee who might do their job? How long would you continue to pay these people without seeing results? I paid the dating industry for ten years, and it never even delivered one relationship on the dollar. It gave me a whole lot of disappointment, shitty treatment, and exposure to microtraumas, though, so I suppose I walked away with something.

How could this be working? How could an entire industry make literal billions without having to actually deliver the thing its customers want?

There's a really simple reason, and put on your self-forgiveness hats to understand it: it's hope. The dating industry knows single women have hope, and it milks that hope for every dollar it's worth. Because we're never supposed to give up hope, right? That'll make us even *more* sad and angry and pity-worthy, geez! We have to hang on to our hope, no matter what, because "giving up" is terrifying, and the dating industry needs job security.

It's easy to take advantage of hope when it's paired with things like helplessness, exhaustion, frustration, desperation, and a blindness to any value or joy in singlehood itself. If being single is the worst thing ever to you, and you have a genuine hope of finding love one day, you are the dating industry's target market, and it loves you very much.

The dating industry gets away with what it's doing because it can. At what point is it ever called out on its bullshit? Is the dating industry ever held accountable for stringing a generation of singles along on maybes, or do new and more dating services and products pop up all the time, capitalizing on the countless singles who will do and pay anything to not be single anymore, regardless of whether or not anything ever actually fucking works?

Why do you think this book exists? Why do you think I took the time to write it? If I can help single women stop seeing singlehood as something bad, a problem to fix, a lower life status, and a horror to avoid at all costs, then things like the dating industry lose their power to fuck with our lives. It's hard to sell your expensive dating service to a woman who doesn't hate being single. It's also entirely possible for someone who has never spent a dime on the dating industry to meet and fall in love with the most significant partner of their life.

I don't like people being taken advantage of—particularly not when they're single women groomed to fear, hate, and be ashamed of their own singlehood by a society that turned around and started charging money to help them "fix" it. Then, to really twist the bra strap, the industry never has to actually *deliver* the one thing society has always held out as the solution to the singlehood it shames us for: a relationship. You're goddamned right I want to be Batman.

You have agency here. You are not an object the dating industry can play with as it pleases. You get to make choices, you get to decide where and how to spend your money, and you get to decide when you're sick of the dating industry's shit. As I've mentioned already, you don't have to cling to the old narratives, or cling to dating culture itself, in order to be worthy of and able to connect with your future relationships. The way to "find love" might *never* be through an industry that doesn't have to actually deliver love but still gets to make money anyway. We need to start acknowledging that possibility.

I'd like to walk through a few of the dating industry's common channels, so if you'd like to participate in the future, you're more equipped to feel in control, rather than strung along to infinity. Let me be clear: you don't need any of this—no one does. You are worthy and deserving of love right this second, just as you are. There is nothing about you that you need to "fix" in order to be "ready" for love. There is no skill or tool you're lacking that's preventing you from finding the right relationships for you. Those of us who are single and want partners are single because we haven't met those partners yet. That's literally the only reason, and all of these players in the dating industry are simply selling maybes.

MATCHMAKERS

A family member once threatened to post on my Facebook page that they were looking for a matchmaker for me if I didn't find and go to one myself. This was back when I lived a life of single shame and also allowed other people to invade my boundaries and influence my behavior. I'm happy to report that neither is true today.

I found a matchmaker, went to visit her, let her tick boxes off on a clipboard during a thirty-minute conversation, and then received an email half a day later letting me know she'd take me on as a client if I gave her $10,000. For that money, she could guarantee me six dates. Six dates—not relationships, dates. For ten grand. This was many years ago, and I have it on good authority that prices have gone up.

Matchmaking as I'm discussing it here as part of the modern dating industry is very different from traditional matchmaking that has led to countless couples and families throughout many cultures and many centuries—and still does. Right now, I'm speaking about mainstream, secular matchmaking services, as opposed to matchmakers within any specific culture or religion. These services vary wildly in terms of pricing and what's included. Anyone using matchmaking needs to be sure they're comfortable with the price and the kinds of maybes involved with each individual matchmaker or service. I was not—nor, thankfully, was my family member.

A more recent example is a friend who received a message from a matchmaking service via LinkedIn. They let her know they'd just *love* to add her to their database of single women, but when she inquired further, they actually wanted to charge her $15,000 to show her photos of five men and see if she wanted to go out with any of them.

One very large glass of wine later, I stopped screaming and helped her come up with a counteroffer. At first, making a counteroffer seemed crazy to her, until I reminded her the service approached her first. She's a thirty-nine-year-old successful attorney who is beautiful, driven, and genuinely amazing company as a friend. This matchmaking service needs women like her far more than she will ever need it. She was not without bargaining chips, but she'd been taught not to use them, because people selling maybes to single women are always presumed to be in the place of power. I see them as power*less* without *us*, so let's fucking negotiate.

She and I settled on the following as her terms: She'd pay them a $1,500 stipend up front to retain their services, and then a $3,000 fee after they'd shown her five men that she actually wanted to meet in person *and* those dates had been arranged. Three months after those dates had taken place, if she was still dating any of those men, she would pay the balance of the $15,000 fee. Two years following that payment, if she was not engaged to marry one of the five men they'd facilitated an introduction to, she would receive 50 percent of her investment back. All of the following would be required in writing. And if they didn't agree, she'd walk away. Because she could.

What are matchmakers selling, really? Are they there for you to just meet potential partners, or are they there for you to stop having to meet any more potential partners in the future? Hold the players in the dating industry accountable. Make them deliver on your investment—or give you your worthless investment *back*. Stop paying for maybes and letting other people get rich while you stay exactly the same amount of single.

(I see nothing wrong with singlehood, but I understand for the sake of argument here that we're paying people *not* to be anymore. That's fine. I'm not trying to kill your optimism or desire; I'm trying to murder their profit margins.)

DATING APPS

I'm going to keep this one brief, because it deserves and receives its own chapter later. For now, though, I'll touch on dating apps because they're by far the most common way single women spend their money on maybes, so they're also the players in the dating industry making the most money. While the expense of matchmakers excludes a significant portion of the single population, the relative affordability of dating apps means anyone can play. These apps have an unfathomably large pool of people to market to and collect fees from.

How much money, over how many years, do you think you've given to dating apps? Forgive yourself for all of it. For every penny. Self-forgiveness is the only way to move forward from a place of learning and positivity. Also, please remember dating apps are businesses specifically designed to relieve you of your money. They're almost a gambling model, and it's possible to sometimes feel addicted to the chance of "finding someone." If you've ever felt like you *had to* keep paying them money or you'd be single forever, that was by design.

Dating apps take your money but never have to guarantee you a damn thing in return. We keep participating, and keep buying in, because the maybe they're selling is one of the most supposedly valuable maybes that exists. Of *course*, we buy in. The maybe seems worth it. But it doesn't have to remain indefinitely worth it without some kind of tangible return on investment.

We all get a little brainwashed now and then—it's okay. Believe me: I know the feeling. I was sucked into the dating app maelstrom for over a decade. You are allowed to stop using dating apps, and you should understand doing so is the very last thing these money-making maybe farms want. The worst thing that could happen to a dating app is for you to meet someone and delete it.

I'll say that again: the worst thing that could happen to a dating app is for you to meet someone and delete it. That's when it stops making money off of you. So what incentive does an app ever have to make sure its product is effective, or that you're treated well while you use it? There are many reasons why dating apps don't belong on our phones, but I like to think this is one of my heavy hitters.

We're scared to stop. We're scared to stop spending the money, and we're scared to stop trying. Because what if he's just one swipe away? What if he's one more paid "boost" away from seeing you and falling in love with you? You choose how long you want to sit at life's little slot machine, thinking what you're after is just a little more money away. Remember that the apps are designed to keep you using them, so they've convinced you that *not* using them is the same thing as choosing to fuck up your romantic future entirely.

Dating apps are for-profit businesses. They're not designed for the people who actually meet their partners. They're designed to continually make money off those of us who never do.

I think it's time we asked ourselves what *exactly* dating apps have contributed to our lives so far. Please know that walking away from dating apps and the maybes they sell you isn't "lowering your chances" if they never once delivered on any of the chances or dollars you gave them in the first place.

DATING ADVICE NEWSLETTERS, BOOKS, ETC.

If you can make it, you can make it about dating advice. Dating advice is always so comical to me. Those giving dating advice like to hide behind the idea of helping people with their insecurities, but then why not call it social advice, life advice, or insecurities advice? They call it "dating advice" because the word "dating" implies, "This will fix your singlehood." They count on the things we associate with dating—like relationships and love—drawing in people and their credit card information like bugs to the zapper.

The reason I don't like "dating advice" is because it can never tell single people the only thing they actually need to know in order to find partnership: when and where to meet their partner. All the "how to be better at dating" advice, whatever it is, assumes you've met someone to go on a date with in the first place. What if you haven't? What if you can't?

Can you get advice on feeling more confident during a date? Sure. (I mean, let's ignore that however you feel when you date is valid and can never scare away the right people for you, but sure.) Can you get advice on where to *find humans to date*? No. And don't say dating apps. I used dating apps for ten years and never had one relationship result from them. With each passing year, booking actual dates with actual humans was increasingly like trying to catch a grain of sand in the ocean during a tropical storm. Blow smoke up someone else's app—I am not the one.

Dating advice can't solve singlehood; it can only provide a mythical crutch that helps singles think they're setting themselves up for success. But there's no piece of advice that can make two people meet, and there's no piece of advice that can make two people fall in love. Following advice can only ever make you feel like you're "doing something" about your singlehood "problem." Dating advice thrives and makes money because single people hate singlehood so much that they can't just "do nothing" about it. Maybe instead of feeding the dating industry money, you can start feeding yourself all the positive parts of singlehood instead. That's free.

"But wait, Shani—didn't you just sell me, a single person, something that costs money? This very book?"

I sure did. But instead of peddling the idea that this book can help you find love, because I'm not in charge of that for you, I'm hopefully helping singles rewrite the way we view *singlehood itself* so that "finding love" becomes less of a panic mode.

I'm never going to try to teach you how to stop wanting a relationship. Please shed that fear as you move through this book. Want relationships—I do! It would just also be amazing if we could want our single lives, too, because those are what we already have, and we don't deserve to hate this time in our lives. We don't deserve to be convinced to hate something that isn't actually bad, so that we can fit into society's boxes or spend thousands of our dollars trying to.

Even when you find a relationship, that won't be what makes you feel good about being single. You'll still hate and fear it and possibly even stay in a bad relationship just to avoid it. However, coming to see the value of singlehood might actually help you feel good *right now*—not *only* when you find a partner you think finally makes you valid. You're valid—and valuable—right now. Also, I hope this book looks nice on your shelf.

Within dating advice books and newsletters are countless methods, tips, tricks, and other suggestions that love to make single people think that luck, fate, and the freedom simply to live our lives and meet people without spending money are romantic fantasies that never come true. They're designed to make us think we need the thing they're selling, unless we want to be single forever (scary!). They're doing a few things here:

1. They're reiterating the assumption that singlehood is a bad, shameful thing. If their "cure" exists, by default your "problem" must exist, too. We internalize this wrongness to the detriment of our

self-esteem. The real kicker: new resources come out all the time—and have been coming out for decades. What message do you think all these dating advice resources for singles send about who we are? If we were acceptable and good as we are now, the resources to change us wouldn't exist.

2. They're trying to sell you on methods for dating that never, at any time, have to actually work— remember that it's all a maybe. Authors and creators will sometimes use their own married status as "proof" that their methods work, even if they met their partner organically and with zero effort whatsoever. In terms of maybes, books and newsletters are the cheapest, but I despise them all the same.

3. Most importantly, they're selling you the idea that you really need to change something about the way you are or the way you operate, and if you just do things their way, *that's* when you'll find someone. If you don't find someone, they get to blame you for not trying hard enough or adhering to their methods correctly, rather than their methods for being faulty in the first place, which I find really fucking convenient.

Dating advice is written from a place of urgency, a place that assumes and reiterates that singlehood is wrong—and you should really be doing something about it. It helps create a problem and then sells you a supposed solution for it. I hate dating advice. No, actually, that's not strong enough. I loathe it entirely.

DATING COACHES

Lord, okay. I'm going to lose friends here, but it's okay for me to disagree with someone's chosen profession if I think that profession is taking advantage of single women.

Coaching is much the same as dating advice books and the like. In some ways, dating coaches are doing something great. If someone is having trouble with social anxiety, confidence, or something else they need help to work through for themselves, great—I'm glad they're not going it alone, and in no way do I think single people should go through everything alone. I'm a huge proponent of singles finding community, friendship, and support at every opportunity. Licensed therapists are also a wonderful resource here. But again, dating coaches call it "dating coaching," not social or confidence coaching, because the word "dating" is a bigger draw for new clients.

The maybes of dating coaching come in again because none of these coaches can tell you where and when to meet your partner. They're not psychic. They can give you all the tips and tricks you want, but at the end of the day, if an actual human partner is what you want, *that's not what they're selling*. They are selling something different, and I'm so sick and tired of the maybes that single people pay for. I want us to start demanding to know exactly what we get for our money.

Dating coaches love to create a glossy deck full of all the things included in their coaching "packages." These packages can run from a few hundred to a few thousand dollars, and please remember you're most likely not going to be married at the end of it. Get clear, very clear, on exactly what you're paying for, and make sure you're comfortable with what you're going to have after working with a dating coach that you didn't have before. Don't be afraid to make them tell you. This is *your money*, and there are enough imbalanced constraints on single-income households without single people thinking they're paying for partnership and getting a journal prompt instead.

I'm not saying never work with a dating coach. If you want to do it, go for it. Just be crystal clear on what your money is buying, and then ask yourself if it's worth that money to you. It's okay to ask a dating coach, "How is your coaching package going to help me meet my partner?" if what you actually want is to meet your partner. Ask them for what they'd consider to be their "success stories," and then ask them how those success stories actually met someone. Was that meeting a direct result of working with the dating coach? My guess is no, unless the coach introduced them, which would make that person a matchmaker, and you already know my thoughts there.

Remember you can never, ever recreate the exact scenario in which two people met. I don't say that to discourage you. I say it because if people can meet in literally any way possible (and they can), it should be easier for you to remember that any way possible can also happen to you. For free.

You shouldn't have to dig for the value of a dating coach's work, because they're the ones selling it. Make them demonstrate to you how their work is worth your money. You are allowed to say no and walk away at any time, and you're also allowed to negotiate. Remember that single people are not lesser beings. We have agency and value just like everyone else does. If they want your money, make them earn it—and if at the end of your work together you're left with *nothing more* than what you had before, get your money the fuck back.

Stop paying for maybes and spending your money because you're desperate for something to "work." I never use the "d" word lightly. This entire book exists because I see a generation, if not multiple generations, of desperate single women who *just want to find someone already!* That singular focus on the one thing we don't have keeps us blind to everything that's already abundant in our lives. When you shift that focus to the genuine value of singlehood, you release the pressure valve on desperation and longing. You might also save a dollar or two.

You don't have to stop wanting something altogether to stop wanting it so badly that you waste your money. My fear is that no amount of money can lead you to the exact time and place you'll meet your partner, but the dating industry will keep collecting cash from you nonetheless.

A major thing to watch out for in any channel within this industry is the married person who uses their married status as a selling point. Honey, you got married one time and you met your husband on a ski trip—how precisely does that make you an expert on helping other people "find love?" While married people can certainly make amazing life and *relationship* coaches, please be wary of any married person in the dating industry if they're using their own married status to bolster their qualifications as someone who can help you find marriage. Doing something once doesn't make you an expert at that thing. They met their partner just like everyone else meets their partner, when luck, fate, chance, timing, etc. aligned for that meeting to happen. It's the same way you'll meet a partner if you want to, and no one is selling a map to the moment it happens. Because they can't.

It's not that I don't want these businesses and products to exist. It's that I want them to be honest. I want them to be respectful. I want there to be consequences when single people feel like they receive nothing real for their money. Peddling the potential of love to a cohort of people who don't have it, and who are further shamed and belittled by society for not having it, isn't an honest industry to me. But it's a thriving one nonetheless, until we decide that we deserve so much more than maybes.

Old thought: *If I don't hire a matchmaker, or use a dating app, or get a dating coach, I'll be single forever.*

New thought: When I stop being single, the dating industry stops making money off of me. Why would the dating industry ever want me to stop being single if my being single is how it makes money? Why would it ever be incentivized to actually connect me with a partner?
Even better new thought: *Falling in love is unpredictable, unplannable, and free.*

There's something you get to have other than hope that's easy to exploit. You also get to have happiness, in such volume that it lives in balance with your hope, and insulates you from feeling helpless. That place where hope and helplessness meet is where the dating industry thrives. When you can reframe your own singlehood to see its value and what a precious time in your life this is, dating apps, coaches, and products lose their power. Suddenly, you don't feel desperate to fix your singlehood, and it's much harder for them to get your money.

How long have you been paying the dating industry for maybes? I don't ask you this to cause you shame. I ask to prompt reflection. When we acknowledge and reflect, we can change our minds. It's okay to look back on the time, effort, and money you've given to the dating industry and evaluate the returns you've seen on your investments. If you don't like what you've received, it is 100 percent your right and within your capability to cut that industry entirely off.

5

A Prologue Life

When you're single, especially when you're single longer or later in life than you ever thought you'd be, there can be a notion that your life hasn't "started" yet. It's as if you're waiting for the "real" part of life to start when you have a partner. These feelings can get compounded when you see everyone around you achieve that "realness" while you're left behind. I used to refer to this feeling as being chained to the starting line of life, while all my friends ran laps around me as they got partnered, engaged, and married.

Of course, this feeling happens. It's just one more extension of singlehood as a societal frown-upon, and we've been avoiding those our entire lives. We graduated high school like we were supposed to, probably went to college like we were supposed to, got a job like we were supposed to—what's next? *Riiiiight*, find the love of your life, get married, have kids, retire, die, the end.

Once we finish a childhood, adolescence, and young adulthood full of instructions and expectations rewarded with acceptance, praise, and the idea that we did what we were "supposed to," why wouldn't we naturally assume the next thing on our list would make our lives valid, just like all the other milestones did? Why wouldn't the absence of that accomplishment make us feel less than? It all seems like a pretty natural outcome to me, one that is certainly ripe for reframing.

This feeling of not being real yet can lead to us living what I call a Prologue Life, or a life that we feel hasn't actually started. It's a life influenced by the ingrained idea that nothing can *really* begin until you have a partner. It is, essentially, living less.

There's no shame in feeling this way, and there's no shame in acknowledging we're doing what we were programmed to. When I realized how much time I'd spent living a Prologue Life, I felt pretty bad about myself—but that feeling dissipated quickly once I bought myself a Cuisinart. Stay with me, I'll explain in a minute.

If you have shame for not feeling quite "real" yet, or maybe not even fully adult yet without a partner, remember where we even got the notion of how life was supposed to go. It wasn't like we grew up thinking that when you turn twenty-five you get issued an iguana and a harp as indicators you'd successfully done adulthood. No, obviously we were all told you "grow up and get married." Our families, peers, media, and very existence as members of modern society baked this expectation into us. We came by this idea honestly, and we'd never had much reason or motivation to challenge it, because it sounded nice! Growing up and getting married sounds nice—it's allowed to. But its absence doesn't have permission to make you feel like shit.

For those of us who grew up but didn't get married (fast enough), it's easy to feel like we failed. It's easy to feel like we're lacking something we're supposed to have, that everyone else has—and if we couldn't find the thing everyone else found, there must be something wrong with us. There isn't, obviously, but these feelings are valid, and it's okay to acknowledge them. I love acknowledging embarrassing or shameful feelings, because it brings them into the light. When they're in the light, we can evaluate them and see how true they really are. If they're not true, we get to let them go. So many notions about singlehood are outdated and essentially *lying*, and I see no value to this community in continuing those falsehoods, so let's rip 'em apart.

There's nothing wrong with us just because we're not married yet or ever. Life is allowed to have timelines of all kinds, not *only* the one where you get married in your late twenties, have two kids by thirty-five, and then raise them until they can vote. We get to put our own spin on life, thank goodness.

Maybe you get married when you're forty. Or fifty. Not because you were "focusing on your career," as if women can't possibly give attention to multiple aspects of their lives, but simply because that's what happened. That's when you met your partner. Why is that considered late? Why isn't it just...fine?

Regarding children and biology, I see and hear you. But the way our world looks at a forty-year-old man getting married for the first time versus a woman doing the same thing—independent of procreation as a factor—is a problem I think I *can* address, whereas parenthood planning is its own highly personal topic. There is an unfathomable amount of unfairness for women who want to have children and simply cannot find a partner to fulfill their parenthood goals with, as if dating isn't difficult enough. I wish things were different. I wish it wasn't this hard to find someone to start a family with. There is nothing I can say that will make it fairer, but I can direct you to the work of Jody Day of Gateway Women, who addresses this topic brilliantly.

Even with the knowledge that we're allowed to live life on a unique timeline, the feelings of shame can remain, and society certainly backs those up by centering our singlehood at every opportunity. The shame is what I believe keeps us in a Prologue Life. Over time, living a life that doesn't feel real can lead to so much smallness. It can lead to us prioritizing other people over ourselves, certainly prioritizing couples over ourselves, and that priority is a lie. We are just as valid, worthy, and real as anyone else, but because we didn't partner up on the expected timeline, we're somehow not actual adults yet.

I love reframing thoughts around singlehood; I think it's the fastest way for single women to feel better. If you'd ever like to do more reframing—about basically everything— look into the work of Kara Loewentheil and her outstanding podcast, *Unf*ck Your Brain*. What I want you to reframe right now is the misconception that "taking so long" to find a partner, or being single far longer into your adulthood than you thought you'd be, is a bad thing. Because what if it's not?

Maybe our lives and timelines looking different is actually a good thing. Isn't that allowed? Maybe our lives are more customized to us than we realize. For example, can you imagine being married to someone you were dating at twenty-two? At twenty-five? At twenty-eight? Would the version of you that you were then honestly still want to be married to a person from that time in your life? Account for how you've grown and developed, and maybe acknowledge that starting a relationship a little later than we were groomed to might actually be a great thing. The older I get, the more I like the idea.

In my younger years, I remember being *so* sad any time I broke up with someone, only to eventually realize what a blessing all those breakups were. The amount of gratitude I have that I never married literally *anyone* I've ever dated is staggering. And if something like time can show me such value, why in the hell would I be angry at the length of time I've been single? Why would I fear more time being single, if I can see all the good it's given me?

When I can look at my thirty-nine-year-old life and my thirteen-year singlehood and spin those things around to see them from another angle, I realize a lengthy singlehood wasn't a punishment or a failure—it was a gift. Maybe I wasn't being held back from partnership that whole time; maybe I was being protected from partnerships that weren't right for me. When I look at my singlehood as a time of protection, rather than one of lack, I am more and more grateful for every *single* day of my life.

A big contributor to a Prologue Life is imbalance. When we hold one aspect of life out as the *most* important, we often dull the rest of life to matter less. There is no question our society prizes partnership and marriage more than anything else, and we can see that in the way marriages are celebrated, revered, and pursued.

When your primary focus is finding partnership, and you spend potentially *years* not finding it, that can leave you with some pretty low feelings. However, if the importance of and focus on finding partnership were on par with other areas of your life, you might not feel as low, because your life would have more balance. If there's "nothing going on" in the romantic area of your life, and you've centered that area above everything else, it's really easy to feel like there's nothing going on in your life at all.

The casual, almost reflex-like centering of dating and partnering is a core component of a Prologue Life that I don't think we take the time to address. What if your *whole life* could work instead, right now, without you having to find a partner first?

You know what centering "finding someone" feels like. Every achievement burns a little less brightly, because we "don't have someone to share it with." It breaks my heart that the accomplishments of single women could somehow be dulled because we don't have a second person by our side to put our arms around in the photos. Put your arm around your raise, your promotion, your dissertation, your house, your health, or your dog. Whatever it is, please don't think the things you accomplish matter less because you accomplished them while single. If you really need someone, know you're sharing your accomplishments with an entire global community of single women who are tired of couplehood receiving the lion's share of celebration— and *we* don't steal the covers.

A consequence of exalting something to the heights to which we lift partnership places us on what I call the Hope Rollercoaster. It's what happens when partnership is the most important thing in our lives. That desperate need to not be single anymore leads us to hang our hopes on anything from first dates, to casual acquaintances, to even pure fantasies, because we want partnership more than *anything*. Every single time we see a potential partner, be it in passing, on an app, or on a date, we get our hopes up *much* higher than we should. Nothing feels better than having "something going on" in the romantic area of our lives, because that's the area we've decided matters more than any other. This is imbalance.

We get excited about someone new, then nothing ever happens, or it fizzles out, or the date goes nowhere, or we get ghosted—and then our hopes crash, hard. A first date you never hear from again might have the capacity to leave you genuinely hurt and upset—for a *while*. It's happened to me, tons of times! I'm not talking out of my ass, I'm talking out of my *memories*.

I've also seen single women get genuinely upset about pure fantasies. Again, no shame. The guy we make eye contact with at the gym all the time will suddenly meet up with his girlfriend in the parking lot, and all the fantasies in our heads about him abruptly die, leaving us crushed, even though we didn't know his name. Because even pure fantasy feels better than having "nothing going on" in our romantic lives. I think it's important to ask ourselves what's actually happening in these scenarios, and then ask ourselves if our hopes and feelings make sense in light of reality. Fantasies are perfectly healthy, but attaching real hopes to them when we've made the romantic area of our lives the *most* important one is another story.

When dating and "finding someone" claim too much of our lives, every single thing we do can potentially be seen as a romantic opportunity. We treat every waking moment like a chance to meet someone, and then our emotions come crashing down when nothing romantic happens. We rarely address this up and down, up and down to see if it even belongs in our lives. We just keep pushing through, over and over, thinking our partner is just a little more effort away. This doesn't sound like very good self-care to me.

I'm not saying don't get excited about dates ever. I'm saying find more balance. Balance the importance with which you view all the different parts of your life, and stop giving one part of life the power to control so much of what you do and how you feel.

There are other, sometimes much more tangible, consequences of believing you're not real yet just because you're single, and they can keep you missing out on so much. In my experience, this manifests in home furnishings.

In addition to feeling like we failed, the Prologue Life can also make us feel like we have to wait. Specifically, that we have to wait for permission, a.k.a. a partner, to do and have the things we want. We don't think we're "allowed" certain things until we've ticked partnership off the list. We think we cannot do or obtain so many things we're looking forward to in life if we're alone.

I think we have this habit of waiting for permission because somewhere inside, we're still trying to be "good" and fit into society, similar to the way we obeyed rules as kids. We're waiting for permission to live the *real* life we've been groomed to believe partnership gives us. The truth is, we're grown adults with bills and jobs—we don't have to wait for a damned thing.

Singlehood behaviors can get weird. And before I go further, let me tell you that I have done the weirdest shit there is to do. Sometimes, and let's keep this between us, I still do it. As I type this to you now, I'm staring at the last shitty couch I will ever have. I bought it when I was still afraid to have nice things. I used to think all I could have was a shitty couch, because "when I meet someone" and we move in together, *what if he doesn't liiiiiiike ittttttt* and then I have to get rid of a nice couch I paid good money for? Or why bother getting a nice couch now when I can get an even *nicer* one when I'm splitting it with someone? I lived this way for *years, you guys!* I was literally buying the cheapest possible furniture for a decade and a half because I was always planning to have better versions of everything when I got married. That's how deep the Prologue Life can go.

The couches were temporary because I thought my life was, too. I thought I was just living in the prologue, the part before my "real life," so why would I need "real" furniture? Too often, we see singlehood as temporary. It's so easy for us to internalize the message of temporariness and adopt it as our own. Singlehood is something we *want* to be temporary—and that's fine! Singlehood can be temporary. But when you let your romantic status be the most important part of yourself, your whole life starts to feel temporary, and that's not cool.

Shedding the notion that the way we live now is temporary can be scary, because we equate doing so with "choosing singlehood," possibly forever—but again, I want to remind you that you don't have to stop wanting a relationship to start loving your single life. The two can coexist, so try it. Try viewing your life right now as solid, and valid, not simply as a waiting period prior to partnership. See what it feels like, and see what it inspires you to do.

Sometimes, the Universe gives you hints that you're on the right track in life. The day I sat down to write this chapter was also the day I had an appointment to go to a showroom to pick out my new, fantastic, kind-of-expensive couch. Every time I sit on it (or lounge on it in a satin robe while drinking champagne—let's live), I will remember how good it feels to acknowledge that my life is real.

What other real do we wait for? In my opinion, pretty much anything you'd find on a wedding registry. I told you we'd get around to my Cuisinart. I cannot tell you how many years I spent cooking and baking (two of my favorite hobbies) while using bad knives, plastic bowls I'd had since college, bent and rusty sheet trays—you name it. If I was going to register for it someday, what was the point in buying the nice version now? I was literally living years of my life surrounded by crappy versions of things just to avoid already having nice versions of them when I got married. Honestly, how many actions have single women taken in service of not having two good blenders someday?

As an aside, one of my best friends in the world also loves to cook and bake. She never really troubled herself with a Prologue Life, so she always bought herself "real" versions of things. She met her now-husband when she was thirty-six, and when they moved in together, they did have multiples of several things around the house. So you know what they did? They had a fucking garage sale. Things work out. Buy a mixer.

You don't need a wedding registry to have nice things. You don't need a partner to rent or buy the home you want.

(Finances permitting, but after running a Facebook group for single women for several years, let me tell you...we buy property.) The hesitation goes back to our thinking we need permission to live fully and do the things we were taught to believe we could only do in partnership. You can do whatever you want, whenever you want, and that will maybe never be more true than right now, when you're single.

My biggest embarrassment around "saving it for when I'm married" was travel. For so many years, I didn't even let the notion of solo travel enter my mind as a possibility. I literally didn't think you could travel alone—I didn't think it was allowed. It was almost like brainwashing. I'd buried the idea of traveling without someone so far down that my mind never saw it as an option. I was way too focused on finding someone so that I'd have someone to travel *with*.

Finally, after one too many Instagrams of other people's vacations, I cracked—into many, many pieces. My thoughts and emotions were shattering my old beliefs about what I was "allowed" to do as a single person. I instantly booked a train ticket to Washington, D.C. (I was living in Brooklyn at the time), and I decided this mini trip would be my litmus test for solo travel. I actually wanted to go to Paris, but... baby steps.

I was terrified the entire time! Nothing scary was happening; I was actually having a really lovely experience, but my anxiety was absolutely peaking. Anything from staring at a painting in a museum to sitting at a bar sipping a drink caused me constant, crippling anxiety.

Is everyone looking at me?

Do they think it's sad that I'm alone?

How am I going to have dinner at a nice restaurant by myself? Isn't that so embarrassing?

These are just samples of the self-loathing thoughts I had in my head. I had to get through them and go on that trip, to prove to myself that I could. I needed to show myself that I could travel alone, that it was possible and allowed, because once I accomplished something previously impossible, the world was next. No one was looking at me. No one thought I was sad. Only *I* thought so, because I thought *they* thought so. Going on my first solo trip helped me see the falsehoods that were keeping me home and how much the imagined opinions of others were affecting my actual life.

We don't need permission to exist, and we don't need permission to "start our lives." You are enough, you are worthy, and you are real. Whatever you've been saving for partnership, know that partnership isn't a prerequisite for it. We have the ability and agency to give permission to ourselves, and the things we get to experience as a result and enjoy in our day-to-day lives are far too lovely to wait for.

So stop waiting. Take the trip to Italy. Get the couch. Replace your shitty toaster. Do the things you thought you had to wait for, because there aren't actually any rules saying you can't. You have your own permission to do whatever the hell you want. This life is not a prologue. It is real, and it is precious and valuable. We are allowed to live like it.

6

Why Are You Single?

You never have to answer this question—I want you to know that. The presence of a question does not demand your compliance with an answer. If you want to just stare blankly into the face of the person who asked it until they walk away from you, that is your right. You never, ever have to answer, "Why are you single?" and anyone asking it should be ashamed of themselves. Yes, I said ashamed of themselves. Given all the shame society's been throwing our way over the years, I think it's perfectly acceptable for me to volley one back in their direction.

There's nothing that stings quite like, "Why are you single?" or, "How are you still single?" when you're the actual single person someone has the audacity to address this way. I wish 100 percent of us would reply with, "I don't know, how are you married?" but this topic is a little more layered.

The question itself implies a negative. It implies singlehood is wrong. It's not like they're saying, "OMG, I wanna be single just like you—tell me your secrets!" No, they're asking it in an accusatory, lacking tone. That's why the question hurts so much: it's the negative motivation behind it. Singlehood is viewed as a wrong state, and when someone sees something wrong, they want to know why the wrong thing is happening, especially when they can't understand how the wrong thing could possibly be happening in the first place. So we get statements like, "I can't believe you're still single!" Only people who haven't dated since college ever ask this question, by the way. When they ask this, or something like it, their cluelessness is showing.

Before we get into the reason this question exists, or why it's still enjoying such prevalence in the discussion around single women, I want to talk strategy. I know that when someone asks us an invasive question, it puts us on the spot and makes us uncomfortable, especially in a group setting. In those moments, it can be hard to think of the response we really want to give, so we fall back on common standbys like a shoulder shrug, a simple "I don't know," or some other placating answer that's usually rewarded with unsolicited dating advice. It's only much later that we realize what we wish we could have said, and by then it's too late.

It's possible to prepare ourselves better for this question and to have a list of answers ready when the time comes. I enjoy the confidence that comes with foresight. My goal is to eradicate "Why are you single?" from the earth, but that might take a while, and I don't want to leave you with nothing while we wait.

My absolute favorite response to this question came from Dr. Kris Marsh when she was a guest on my podcast. While I was writing this book, she was writing *The Love Jones Cohort: Single and Living Alone in the Black Middle Class*. When it comes out, I really hope you'll read it. Dr. Marsh's response to *Why are you single?* is simply: *What do you mean by that?*

Is that not genius?! It swiftly places the focus and responsibility back on the person who asked this dumbass question in the first place. It's glorious—I love it so much. "What do you mean by that?" makes the question-asker think about the question itself, and it does *not take long* for them to realize how rude it actually is.

You also have the option to reject the question outright. You are allowed to say, "I don't answer that question." You don't have to explain your answer or satisfy anyone around you, because *you're* the one who's been placed in an insulting situation here, not them. Don't be afraid of an awkward silence here, as you're not the one who caused it. Let the discomfort pass, and let the person who asked think of something else to say. In this moment, that's not your responsibility.

It's not our chore as single women to make everyone else around us "okay" with our singlehood. We don't have to assure everyone in the room or at the table that we're "fine." They should have understood how we were doing when they asked us, "How are you?" And if they didn't ask how you were before they asked about your relationship status, maybe don't ever hang out with that person again.

Another option is a clean and quick, "Excuse me?" You can even pair it with a little stink eye if you want. This will probably be followed up with, "I just mean, you're so great! I can't believe no one's scooped you up yet!" That old chestnut, to which I would say, "Yeah, me neither!" Because what are you supposed to say?! What's going to make them happy in this scenario? There is no way out of this that will satisfy them and leave you with an ounce of self-worth, so let's not even get into those weeds. Remember that right now, it is *not your responsibility* to dazzle someone with a witty response to their feckless question. It is their responsibility to have a few fucking manners and never ask it again.

If you have the stomach for it, you really can turn the question around on them. You are allowed to ask, "How are you married?" or "How are you in a relationship?" Thats no more an invasion of privacy than the question they just threw your way. Can you imagine sitting down to dinner with a friend and asking them, "How are you married?" They'd probably never want to see you again! All for the crime of making them justify how in the hell they attracted a partner. Never mind the fact that partnered people have been making single people provide reasons for our singlehood forever.

Why am I single? I dunno, Paul, why are you still asking this archaic question? Why are you so bad at small talk? Why can you not come up with anything more interesting in conversation than something that shames single people? Why are we your easy icebreaker? I'm not worried about why I'm single, but I do have concerns about your social skills, pal.

Another question I love, and by "love" I mean utterly despise, is, "So how's dating going?" (I had to go scream into the abyss after I typed that.) You are allowed if not encouraged to respond to this question with, "I don't know—how happy is your marriage?" It's the same damn question. Partnered people don't get to invade the romantic lives of singles any more than we get to invade theirs. Partnered people are not better or more deserving of romantic privacy than single people. We are equal. Stop answering these bullshit questions, you don't have to.

Listen, I know it might be scary to answer, "Why are you single?" in a way that shocks the shit out of the person who mindlessly asked it. It's one of those moments when we don't want to hurt people's feelings even though they hurt ours first. I promise you it gets easier with time and practice, and we can stop seeing it as hurting feelings. We're not intentionally hurting someone; we're protecting ourselves—there's a difference.

If it helps, know that every time you refuse to comply with a typical, "Why are you single?" answer, you're training the person who asked it to never ask it again. So essentially, you're saving your single siblings from having to answer this question in the future. We are in this together, team. Let's help each other out.

I really don't like it when single women answer, "Why are you single?" with actual "reasons." I know how we can see this as empowering, giving the question-asker a taste of how difficult this single life can be, but I think when we answer it with actual reasons like, "Dating is hard!" or, "I'm forty and our patriarchal society only considers women in their twenties desirable!" we're basically playing right into this question's hands.

Answering this question with actual reasons you think you're single gives the question itself more power. These answers *agree* with the question that there's something wrong with being single itself. There isn't, so let's stop giving the question what it wants.

The reasons are bullshit—they're all made up. How many times have you had a quirky friend you thought was single due to their quirk who then got married to someone who loves your friend *because of that quirk* or someone who has the *same damn quirk?* Get out of here with "reasons." Reasons are in the eye of the beholder.

The nonsense of reasons doesn't mean we aren't actually fielding them in our real, single lives. So fine, if society has its "reasons" why we're single, and it thinks it's entitled to ask us to provide one or more of them as an answer to an asinine question, let's get into a few.

YOU'RE TOO PICKY.

Cool Amber, so you met your husband because you... weren't picky? Why do other people get to be picky when it comes to the people they'll spend the rest of their lives with, but anyone who happens to be single later in time than the person using this "reason" is too picky? I guarantee you no one thinks through this reason before they assume it's the secret to why you're "still single." If you're single because you're picky, they're married because they're not. If they come back at you with some nonsense about you "getting older" and needing to lower your standards because of your natural human age, remind them that but for the grace of the divorce rate, they could be right back in singlehood, too—and I wonder how "too picky" would feel as a reason for them then. I genuinely don't care how salty I sound right now. I came by this seasoning honestly.

Telling someone they're picky is the exact same thing as calling them unwantable to their face. A person who says this isn't saying what they really mean. They're just hiding what they really think is wrong with you underneath the word "picky," and they're implying you should take what you can get. The person who tells you you're too picky is not someone adding to your life in a productive way. They're also a person who can't see validity in being single because they've never entertained the idea, and in that sense, I have empathy for them, because that's fucking sad. You're goddamn right I'm picky. I'm not about to share my *whole actual life* with someone just because they were *there*.

YOU'RE NOT TRYING HARD ENOUGH.

What's enough? Because last I checked, and I checked by trying for a decade, effort doesn't match reward in dating.

If you hear this used as a reason, I challenge you to ask the person saying it to give you their definition of "enough." Seriously, what's enough? Enough stops when you meet someone, and everyone meets someone at a different time and place in their lives. So determining that someone isn't trying hard "enough" to find their partner is a really convenient reason to give. The person saying it gets to choose what "enough" is, and I'm sure it'll be "enough" the second you meet your partner. Funny how that works out.

YOU'RE TRYING TOO HARD.

This is the exact opposite of the reason above, probably given to you by the same person who said you weren't trying hard enough three months earlier. I literally can't with this hypocritical shit.

YOU'RE AN ANGRY BITCH.

Okay, this one's personal. I will never, as long as I live, forget the night someone first called me angry. I was out with girlfriends—actual friends of mine—in my second or so year of being single. (Oh, if she only knew what was coming.) I was having a really rough go of dating. It seemed like I'd been on ten disastrous dates in a row, with maybe one or two good dates I never heard from again sprinkled in between. I was venting about this. I actually hate venting. I don't find it to be productive or goal-oriented in any way. If you're going to vent, be intentional about it and ask yourself what you want to get out it. It should be more than "tell someone what happened so they can validate me." Otherwise, you're just putting your shit onto someone else so their mood can come down to match yours, and I think that's mean.

One of my friends replied to my venting with, "Well, of course you're not finding someone—you're so angry!" Telling someone they're angry is so dismissive. It's also invalidating and accusatory—as if the stories from my dating hellscape that I was recounting to friends were the same conversation fodder I used on dates. As if the attitude I adopt in a safe space among friends is the attitude I adopt the first time I meet a stranger. I'm not fucking angry on dates, Tina—I'm just angry *right now*. Let's not translate that to my entire approach to finding partnership, thanks. I swear to you, people will latch on to *anything* if it means they get to think they're right about what your "problem" is.

YOU'RE TOO... SOMETHING.

This all-encompassing "too" reason can go fly a flaming kite. No, single women aren't "too" anything. We aren't too old, too fat, too skinny, too unpretty, too smart, too loud, too opinionated (I've heard this one said to my face on a date), too independent, too needy, too boring, too wild, too tall, too short, too masculine, too feminine, too weird, too normal, too intimidating, too *anything*. You're never too something to be loved by the people who will never need to be persuaded to love you. You know how I know? Because every partnered person I know is "too" something, too.

All of the "toos" we hear in the dating space are just people needing to make themselves feel better about *our* singlehood. Again, people like being right, and people don't like being confused. So if they can't figure out why you're single, they'll pick a reason and feel better. These reasons don't actually have anything to do with you; they have to do with other people's limited beliefs about being single.

Reasons apply when convenient, and people assert them without manners. Reasons put the burden on single women. They assume the "reason" is the thing you need to "work on" in order to not be single anymore. Unfortunately, we can also internalize these messages, and then we start telling ourselves that these reasons are keeping us single, too.

The only reason anyone is still single when they don't want to be is that they haven't met their partner yet. That's it.

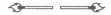

It's very hard to get out of "Why are you single?" without receiving dating advice. Any answer we've previously relied on has always had the unfortunate propensity to suggest we're somehow in need. I'm just curious: when is it enough? When is it time to stop with the tips and tricks and so on? When have we as a whole society had enough dating advice?

When is it time to admit that the dating advice approach isn't working, and that alternatively it's time to look at why we're even interested in advice at all? I honestly write this from a place of exhaustion with dating advice. I think we're oversaturated with it. I'm so truly tired of the very basic assumptions made about single women, so let's reframe:

Old thought: *I'm single, so I must be doing something wrong.*

The couplehood good/singlehood bad assumption is part of what keeps us so ashamed of our singlehood and so dedicated to "fixing" it. I want to talk about how the *only* messaging we seem to be able to give to single women pertains to making us better at dating and supposedly more likely to "find someone." Everything created for single women comes at us as if we're operating at a deficit. Why are we never allowed to just *be what we are?*

New thought: *I'm single.*

Imagine that. Imagine if being single were just a totally okay thing to be, a thing that didn't require extra life effort or solutions. What if being single were just as acceptable, or dare I say just as *celebrated*, as couplehood? I wonder how often we'd be asked why we are what we are in that case.

Have you read any articles, books, or social media posts recently that pertain to any of the following?

- How to Be Better at Dating
- How to Survive Dating

- Best Cities for Dating
- Best Apps for Dating
- Best Places to Go on a Date
- What to Do on a Date
- What Not to Do on a Date
- How to Write a Dating Profile
- What to Do After a Date
- How to Deal with Dating
- How to Interpret Unclear Messages Shitbag Guys Send You After a Date

I could go on, but instead I'd like to ask again: Have you had enough yet? Are you sick of it yet? Has any of it ever actually fucking worked?

Honestly, how many years' worth of dating advice are we going to consume as single women before we start demanding that the world give advice to *someone else?* I think after decades of focusing intently on single women, dating advice has put in the work with that demographic. Instead, I think dating apps, dating culture, and, by god, *single men* deserve some of this shitty spotlight.

Let's first tackle unwanted advice, that old fly in the latte. Unwanted advice most often comes to us over dinner, where a restaurant has inevitably served us a three-piece appetizer that we'll awkwardly have to split between two or four people. (Honestly, why do they do that? It drives me crazy.) Dinners with friends, if you're a single woman, always start the same way: "So, are you *seeeeeeinnngggg anybodyyyyyy?*" And when we say no, because actually finding someone on a dating app that's half-bot and half-dudes you swiped through two years ago already is really hard, whoever we're dining with takes that "no" to mean there's something wrong with the single woman, not with the institution of dating itself.

Dating culture—and certainly the dating industry—continually gets away with being the fucking worst while society blames single women for "doing it wrong"—as if there's a "right" way to do something awful. It's like blaming the fish for dying in a dirty tank.

Ghosting, breadcrumbing, these things shouldn't be allowed to exist, yet they do. It's never the dating apps that have a problem; it's the single women using them. We've just accepted all the bullshit as charming little idiosyncrasies of the culture. Do you think the founders of dating apps ever sit down to dinner and have to answer, "*So...how are you improving your app experience for single womennnnn- nnn?*" Literally never.

You know what really sticks a finger in my frosting? The fact that the people giving dating advice didn't actually have to follow it in order to find a partner. Instead, they probably just had to flirt with the new person on the engineering team for a month until they got asked out. But I digress.

You know I don't like it when people take single women's money and give them a maybe in return. I *also* don't like it when an entire social media culture is stuffed to the rafters with memes and quotes and posts that tell single women everything they're doing wrong, or how to deal with what the dating world is doing wrong, rather than creating content that focuses on telling the *dating industry* to get its shit together. I mean really, can you imagine an Instagram quote that reads: *If every client isn't meeting their partner after working with you, you're not a dating coach. You're someone who knew how to set up a website that collects credit card information.* I'd love to see it.

Single women aren't always the problem, but we are always the primary group of people on the receiving end of advice. How much goddamned advice do people actually think we need? And does the prevalence of the advice tell us nothing? Maybe this much advice for this long should be letting us know that the advice *isn't good*.

I will never forget the last piece of dating advice I took. A dear friend of mine, who also works in the dating space, saw I was having a tough time and told me I had to stop having text-based communications with men. She believed in the power of people connecting with their actual voices and thought texts were taking opportunities for connection away from us. She insisted that *I* insist on making the guy I was texting with at the time call me to set up our next date. I was not allowed to let him book a date via text—I had to say something like, "I'm really busy at work right now—why don't you give me a call tonight and we can make plans?" The phone call lasted two minutes and forty-five seconds, it was the most awkward conversation of my life, and I never saw him again. I haven't listened to dating advice since.

It's not that my friend was wrong *per se*—it's just that in an area of life where effort never has to match reward, advice doesn't *ever* have to produce results, either. Dating advice often has a lot to do with the advice-giver deciding what our "problem" is and then tailoring their advice to their thoughts, rather than to our actual experiences. It's about as solid as predicting the future or guessing how many fingers someone's holding up behind their back. It's a risk-free situation for the advice-giver. If they're right, they're a hero. If they're wrong, the single person didn't follow the advice correctly, or some other equally conse-quence-less outcome for the person giving the advice.

As singles, we have a bad habit of doing the same things over and over again (hello, swiping) because we assume that one time it's just going to "click." We're allowed to quit before it clicks—and be open to living free of the burden of being wrong all the time. I know the gut reaction to a prob-lem is to find a solution. And I know society has raised us to feel like our singlehood is a problem. So naturally, when we can't seem to find a solution (or partner) to the problem, we'll instinctually reach out for help, wisdom, training— anything that will make singlehood go away. This tendency is why it is so important to me to communicate to single women that our singleness is not actually a problem.

Being single isn't a bad thing; it never was. It isn't an inherently lacking state of being alive. Who you are as an individual can never lack *another person* in order to be valid. When being single isn't itself a bad, wrong thing, maybe we won't feel so driven to seek out advice and ways to "fix" it. This is especially pertinent because none of the advice or help can ever actually tell you where to find your partner.

It's okay if the advice isn't working for you. That doesn't mean something's wrong with you. It might actually mean there's something wrong with the advice itself, and you get to choose to stop listening to it.

We've absorbed enough advice for a lifetime. I don't care how the world thinks I'm contributing to my own singleness, because my singleness isn't something I have to repair. Instead, it's just one part of my valid and amazing life, something I get to live, rather than something I have to make it through in one piece until I find a partner. I think it's time for the world to stop its overabundance of dating advice aimed at single women and maybe point its efforts in another direction. Our shift is over, and it was long.

Instead of, "Hey, single women, here's how to deal with dating!" maybe we could try, "Hey, dating world, here's how to stop being something single women have to deal with!" Anyway, that's my advice.

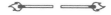

This is probably one of the most heterosexual parts of this book, but it's a situation that's happening, and I think when straight single women don't acknowledge it's happening, we have a harder time. I think when we enter the dating space as single women, not all—but a significant portion of us—are going into it looking for relationships, companionship, and love. I think a similarly significant percentage of single straight men are simply trying to get laid. I also think society shames women's intentions for being ignorant, while it accepts men's intentions as "the way dating is now."

I once let a man know how insulted I was by his dating app message that suggested, in far less delicate terms, that we have casual sex. It was the first thing he said to me after "Hello." His response to my taking offense? "You know what [insert name of dating app] is for, right?" It wasn't his fault for being lewd to a woman; it was her fault for expecting common decency. He was telling me the truth about why men use dating apps, and trying to make me feel stupid for thinking they were intended for anything else. I'll never forget this exchange. It's not the only one like it that I've experienced, and I'm far from the only person it's ever happened to.

I've been made to feel uncool or silly for even attempting to date for serious reasons as opposed to just accepting that all that's out there are people who want to hook up. I don't hook up. I'm not a part of hookup culture. Maybe I was in my twenties (okay, I *definitely* was in my twenties), but that's not who I am anymore. And in the dating space, I've been made to feel like that makes me wrong, boring, or an idiot.

You're not doing something wrong or somehow prolonging your own singlehood simply by taking your singlehood and dating seriously. It's okay if you don't just date "for fun." It's okay if you date with intention, too. I know the world doesn't make you feel very cool for that, but I'm going to try.

I'm sorry we've built a dating culture that punishes us for our certainty. I'm sorry "knowing what we want" has been labeled intimidating, as opposed to what it really is: helpful. If one more person describes me as "no bullshit," I will light the world on fire—I really will. Calling a woman "no bullshit" is the "bless her heart" of the dating world. It implies that my knowing what I want and wanting more than the minimum is an aggressive, imposing way to live. I'm sorry we live and interact in a dating culture where the most intentionless, noncommittal among us are prized, while the most assured among us are made to feel needy, desperate, crazy, or "too much." You are not a plague upon the earth for having valid desires and feelings. You're not wrong. You're the truth.

You are allowed to take dating seriously, and you are allowed to take yourself seriously. You're allowed to approach relationships and partnerships with purpose. You don't have to approach them pretending not to care. If you care, you care, and that's allowed because it's true. Caring is not a negative, but we've been encouraged to think it is—by those who themselves don't care about dating at all and make it pretty damn clear they don't care about us, either. We don't have to adjust our wants and needs to center the most disengaged among us. Not caring won't make you more marriageable. Pretending not to care when you actually do only makes you a liar. Don't lie for these fuckers. They're not worth it.

You aren't uncool for wanting a future. Or a marriage. Or a family. You're allowed to stop wanting a fucking hookup and start acknowledging for yourself that there's nothing lame about you for wanting a real partner. The word "situationship" does not have to exist in your vocabulary. You don't have to be okay with "kind ofs." You can walk away from what is not enough for you, because not enough is not all that will ever show up.

You are worth more than crumbs. You deserve more than tiny encouragements evenly spaced. You don't have to be someone's easy option if you really want to be shown someone's extra effort. You are worth what you want, and I'm sorry we've built a dating culture that communicates otherwise. It is lying.

Discomfort with casual doesn't make you boring—it never did. Anyone who thinks it does has clearly never had anything serious. If serious isn't hot enough for you, you're doing it wrong. In my opinion, it's casual that's far more likely to feel flat. Feelings aren't flaws. Don't let a bullshit system make you feel guilty for what comes naturally to you. Make the system feel guilty for its bullshit instead.

A program will run as it's been coded. We've been coded and trained to come across as free and as breezy as possible, even if we're terrified and lonely and anxious inside. We've been coded to be those things, too, by the very system that makes us feel like idiots for having completely valid feelings. Break the fucking code. Be the glitch. Change the system. Acknowledge and celebrate what you want. Do not settle for anything less. You are worth what you want; do not let the digitization of dating tell you otherwise. The truth of you, the passion of you, the worthiness of you—they're all facts that need no validation or buy-in from those who can't be bothered with the most basic of manners.

Something that already exists doesn't need permission to show up. There's nothing wrong with taking dating seriously, and you're allowed to be fucking *done* with those who don't. You don't have to change what you want in order to fit people who aren't actually your options. The right people for you will want you, period. It won't feel like a stressful game. It will feel like peace. And peace is really fucking cool.

Be your lovable, wantable truth. That will always feel better than pretending to be less or want less—and better than lying to present a false package that a twisted system has told you to be. People don't find love in a system. They find it in life, luck, and truth. I think that's really cool, too.

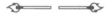

When someone asks, "Why are you single?" what they're really asking is, "What's wrong with you?" The short, and conveniently accurate, answer is: nothing. There is nothing wrong with us that is causing our singleness, just like there's nothing more right about partnered people that makes them partnered. Partnership does not equal perfection. Partnership means compatibility, compromise, trust, and timing. It's not a stamp of approval. It's just a thing that happens in life. Don't let a lack of partnership indicate the presence of personal flaws.

There is one reason, and one reason only, why you and I are "still single:" we haven't met our partners yet. It's no more complicated or involved than that. We haven't met them, but I believe down to my shoes that if we want to, we will. I can't tell you when or how, and I strongly caution against listening to anyone who says otherwise—especially someone who says changing aspects of yourself is the way to make the right partner for you magically appear. You don't have to change anything to be lovable. You already are.

You don't have to validate your existence to someone else by supplying them with an answer to their rude question. You don't have to listen to anyone's advice about something that isn't wrong. You don't have to treat dating like a game if it's not a game to you.

We can choose to stop seeing our singlehood as a set of problems and faults to fix. I'd love to see a world where singlehood and couplehood are enjoyed in equal measure, a world where one status isn't seen as a problem to be reasoned away. I want that world with more urgency than I want a partner, if I'm being honest.

Every now and then, when someone asks, "Why are you single?" you might get a little something extra from them. They might say, "Well, I think you're fantastic. I'm sure there's someone coming along for you any minute now."

While it's a sweet thing to say, I guess, how do they know? Why do they feel they need to say this? Why can't being single just be a good thing? Why is the assurance we'll soon have someone other than ourselves the comforting message, rather than someone letting us know we're whole and valid and enough on our own? I'd so much rather have someone tell me that than try to predict the future for me and tell me what I know is a blatant falsehood.

Singlehood isn't something that has a why, but you are someone who has worth. And the next time someone has bad manners enough to ask you this question, you're allowed to forget your manners, too.

7

It's Not Your Job

.

You don't have to date if you don't enjoy it. I know single women don't hear that very often. Usually, when we complain about dating, instead of really listening to us and seeing a need for change in modern dating culture itself, those not in the shit—and maybe even some who are—simply suggest tips, tricks, and alternate means of *doing* dating instead. People assume that even though dating is making us miserable, trying something different is always better than walking away from it altogether. Right now, I'm not talking to those who love to date. If you love dating, keep dating. If you hate dating, keep reading.

Singlehood and dating aren't short on charming phrases and everyday-isms that we've come to accept as totally okay and true. We're quick to give a dating practice—however abhorrent—a charming name like "ghosting," which is really just being flat-out ignored and forgotten, or "snow-globing," which is...actually, I have no idea what that is but I saw it on Twitter.

One thing we like to say about dating is that it feels like a "second job." Normalizing the actual and emotional work of dating by painting it with a, "Welp, I guess this is the way it's gonna be now!" brush is unacceptable to me. We nickname and accept things that are terrible and unfair, instead of talking about how we can stop the terrible things from happening in the first place.

I'm very, very tired of talking about how bad dating has become without anyone offering ideas or solutions. Dating shouldn't *ever* feel like a second job, because you're not getting paid, you're not developing a career, and you are under no obligation whatsoever to do this kind of work. Dating is *not your job*.

You don't have to date. Has anyone ever told you that singlehood isn't something you have to "do something" about? If you've never been told you're just allowed to just... *live*, please know it's true. I know it sounds scary right now. I'm going to work on that.

There are many problems with modern dating, but one of the biggest is it's just something we *do*. We rarely challenge or evaluate it. We treat it as an assumed, casual to-do list item. If we're single, dating is a thing we do, because we're single, and we can't be single. We have to find someone, and how do you find someone? Date!

Then we date for years. Maybe many, many years. What if it never leads to the thing we always thought it would? How long do you just keep going and "trying to find someone" via dating? How long do you stay on the grind? How long do you feel obligated to? How deeply have you convinced yourself that you can't stop until it works?

Sometimes I worry it doesn't matter how much I applaud the freedom and opportunity that single life affords us or how much I reiterate there's nothing wrong with us just because we happen to be single. Sometimes I think, at the end of the day, everyone just wants a fucking boyfriend.

And that's fine. I want one, too! I think having a partner sounds lovely, and I look forward to it. But modern dating culture isn't the positive experience that was sold to me. It's something much more difficult, punishing, dismissive, and cruel. Anyone who doesn't agree either a) loves dating anyway, or b) clearly hasn't done it recently or from a place of sincerely desiring a partner. It's a disconnect mentally, because the act of two people finding each other logically computes as a good experience but plays out in real life another way.

We never sign up for this thinking all we'll ever get is swiping through a dating app on the toilet for weeks until we find one person willing to go on a date with us, then kissing them goodnight at our door and never hearing a word from them again as if they died. But something in the ballpark of this is what happens anyway. On a *good* day.

I get that dating isn't what we want it to be. What I'm saying is, if it's not what we want it to be, why are we settling for it anyway? Why aren't we walking away from it and pursuing other things in life that make us feel good?

If dating isn't enjoyable, why do we do it? Why do we think we *have to* date?

I once saw an Instagram quote that said, "Being a hopeless romantic stuck in hookup culture is a special kind of hell."

It had thousands of likes and hundreds of comments nodding in agreement. It never dawned on any of these people behaving like social media lemmings to question the logic of the quote. It's like an entire single community has lost free will and believes they're obligated to stay in an environment they hate.

No one's ever "stuck" in hookup culture. You are choosing to be there. You are choosing to put yourself in the current dating world voluntarily. And if you find things you don't like about dating and hookup culture, you are allowed to leave—but do you? I certainly didn't, for a decade. I'm not accusing you of making a bad choice. I'm forgiving us all for behaving exactly as society wants singles to behave, and certainly how a dating industry making money off of us wants us to behave.

Those of us who choose to date but don't vibe with hookup culture might not participate in the casual sex or casual dating that can be so common, and I certainly hope we don't continue to engage with people who have goals vastly different from our own, but we still tend to stay in that world nonetheless. We still keep dating. Why? And why do we view this as us being "stuck" in a dating night-mare? Why don't we see ourselves as beings with free will who can choose to leave?

We don't like to think of dating as a choice. We don't want to acknowledge we have a choice to leave. We just want to complain and bitch and vent about how bad dating is and then go right back to it. I don't help us by denying that this is the pattern we repeat. I'm trying to help us break out of it. I'm not shocked by the things we encounter in modern dating culture. I'm shocked by how many of us still choose to participate.

I'm trying to help singles view singlehood as something *other than* a problem to fix at any cost. Once you start viewing your own singlehood in a reframed light, there is no dating app, no dick pic, no third date ghost who can harm you. That's because you've managed to stop clinging to dating as your ticket out of singlehood. Has that ticket taken you where you want to go yet, or ever? By reframing the way you view and experience your own singlehood, you increase your self-worth around it. You learn what you deserve and what you don't. You don't deserve to stay in a dating space that makes you feel bad. You deserve to abandon it and meet your future partner anyway.

No one wants to hear that we should stop dating if dating makes us unhappy, because we think that means we'll be single forever. In our minds, if we don't date, we'll "never find someone."

Finding someone—my god. It's the driving force. It's the furnace fueling the hope that keeps single people swiping.

Swiping in every spare moment, every unoccupied second, on an unshakable mission to find someone. I used to be on such a mission; I know it well. I would swipe, and swipe, and swipe, and swipe, and swipe—endlessly, and to very little avail. A match once every couple of weeks, a date every few months. And nothing but unanswered messages, lewd advances, and a whole lot of nothingness in between telling me exactly how unwanted I was according to dating culture.

I thought I had to keep going. I thought I had to be in that space, specifically online dating, because there is literally no other easy public format for meeting new single people anymore, and I wanted to meet another single person and then marry them. We don't have dances and socials and shit like they did when our grandparents were courting. All we're left with is the digital face buffet. So romantic.

I thought dating was my only option. I was single, single was bad, and online dating was where the men were. So that's where I was. And I was getting the shit kicked out of me. It was a constant stream of incoming negativity. Either zero matches—which is not nothing by the way, since it's negativity coming at you in the form of constant reinforcement that no one wants you. Or I participated in the lamest of messaging encounters, in which I felt like some kind of jester who had to keep men entertained, lest they be lured away from our conversation by one of fifty others they were currently carrying on. I felt like a toy they got bored of playing with very easily.

I'm grateful for many moments in my life, but the "fuck this" moment I had regarding dating apps might take the biscuit. It was the first time I asked myself, "What have dating apps ever done for me? What have I ever actually gained from dating apps?" What followed changed my life.

The last time I logged on to my dating apps was January 26, 2019, and that was to delete them. That was the day I stopped participating. I decided to remove my dating apps' access to me, because they were making me hate my life. Dating culture doesn't get to do that to me, not when I won't allow it to. I never downloaded the apps again. Better still, I've never even wanted to.

I also stopped venting about the behaviors of men and the failings of dating apps—and other horrors of dating culture—in my writing. Bitching about them into infinity was just giving them more audience and validation. It wasn't solving anything. Men and dating apps never seemed to care how often or how loudly I (and others!) called them out. The behaviors continued. In my experience, they even got worse. But discussing and challenging how single people view their own singleness, while trying to improve it, might actually have legs. If we don't hate being single, we stop being human beings whom dating culture can harm. We cut dating culture off at the source of its power: singlehood shame, lack, and misery. Y'all...it *works*.

I can't tell you how to not feel stuck in dating culture other than to leave it. What I can also tell you is that you're asking the wrong question. Instead of asking yourself why dating sucks so much, ask yourself why you're still dating. "Why is dating so bad?" is no longer the question. Dating culture is bad because we've allowed it to decline in quality without consequence. Worse still, the digitization of dating has given it even *more* opportunity to become a dumpster set aflame. Why it's bad is not the question. Why we stay in it most certainly is.

To continue dating even though you know it doesn't treat you well is prioritizing "finding someone" over your own feelings. If dating is "a special kind of hell" for you, please know you don't have to keep going. You can stop dating. You can remove yourself from the apps and the spaces you don't like, the ones making you feel miserable and frustrated and hopeless. You. Don't. Have. To. Be. There.

Okay, let's just say it: "But...if I don't date...how will I find someone?!"

Can I ask you something? Are you finding someone now?

No one fucking knows how to meet someone. No one can tell you that, ever. And please don't pay anyone who tells you that they can. The incredibly simple answer to "But then how will I meet someone?" is...anywhere. You will meet someone anywhere. I cannot tell you when, or how, but I do know that human beings have been meeting in an infinite number of ways since the dawn of time, and honestly, you're really not an anomaly.

People meet. They just do. They meet at parties, at work, at bars, on airplanes. They meet at conferences, music festivals, and corporate retreats. They meet on the street sometimes! There are literally endless, unfathomably variable ways people meet and come together in life. This is not, by the way, an invitation to treat every time you leave the house like a potential meet-cute. That's not your job either. Take that "you never *knoooowwwwww*" bullshit and shove it where the sun has never shined. Single women are allowed to just *live*. Goddamn.

I have a theory that if you interview 1,000 couples, you will get 1,000 different stories about how they met. I think singles need to hear these stories. As jealousy-inducing and painful as we think they might be, we need to reframe what we're hearing. Let's stop viewing the stories of how people met as further examples of what we *don't have*, and start viewing them as examples of what's *possible*. I want us to remember that anything is possible, and there's a lot more anything out there for us than what we can swipe through.

But you probably don't want to hear that people meet during the normal course of living life, because for some reason it feels better to hear you can just hop on a dating app and control the situation by swiping your way to love. Maybe simply living life and meeting someone during the natural course of existing sounds like it's going to take too much time. I can promise you, when you live a happy single life, you stop looking at the clock.

Just living life without putting in "effort" to find someone feels lazy. It feels like we're not "doing enough." That's because we've been programmed to feel so ashamed of our singlehood that we believe walking away from a punishing dating culture that disappoints and harms us is somehow the failure, instead of acknowledging how the entire dating industry has failed *us*.

No one wants to walk away from the dating shitshow because it'll "lower their chances," but we completely ignore the fact that those chances haven't netted a win yet. Is dating working for you? Has it ever? Is a space that holds itself out to be a solution to your singleness actually serving you in any way, or is it lowering your self-worth one swipe at a time?

Think about it: every time you swipe right and they don't swipe right back, what message is that communicating to you? Every time you message someone and they never respond? Every time you get a message that's inappropriate or unwelcome? How much negativity do you think you've absorbed over time, and what effect do you think it's had on you? Dating app memberships need to come with therapists, but they don't. We don't deserve everything we're taking in from dating culture. We never did.

Is being single really *that bad?* I don't think it is, certainly not bad enough to endure what dating has become. Singlehood itself isn't the miserable thing. As I mentioned, our current dating culture is the miserable thing, and it's letting our singlehood take the blame for how it makes us feel. I don't let it get away with that particular bamboozle anymore.

How far are we willing to go to find someone? I was willing to go for a decade. A decade of pure dating disappointment made my self-worth shrink to the size of a jelly bean and my mental health balance on the tip of a bobby pin. I am currently dating less than I ever have before, and I am currently happier, more creative, more productive, and mentally healthier than I've ever been. I am also more optimistic about my future relationships than I've ever been—imagine that! Dating wasn't working for me, but living sure as shit is.

I don't know how or when I'm going to meet my partner. But the fact that I'm comfortable with not knowing, that I've freed myself from dating as a mandatory chore, is one of the kindest things I've ever done for myself.

I made the decision to center myself instead of my future partnership—because I have me right now, and *I* seem to be the more pressing issue. If swiping through thousands and thousands of faces wasn't bringing me closer to partnership, then why should just living my life and seeing what happens keep me any farther from it?

It isn't a fucking numbers game: it's your life. You are allowed to remove anything from your life that makes you feel bad. Why do we spend more energy searching for someone we don't have than on acknowledging and enjoying who we already are?

You don't have to "swear off dating." There's no rule around that, and no one's asking you to. What I'm suggesting is that you decenter it and remove the staunch reliance on dating to solve a situation that isn't a problem in the first place. It might take baby steps and practice, but putting less effort into something that doesn't need to be fixed is doing yourself a kindness.

Loosen the grip on dating. If you start to feel scared, remember: if all that effort didn't "work" anyway, then what do you have to lose by letting go? Remember that life happens, and relationships are part of life. A culture that makes you miserable will never be your only path to love and partnership. Personally, I have more faith in life and humanity than that.

Single women are allowed to simply live, breathe, and connect with the right relationships for them whenever they happen. We aren't required to endlessly pursue those relationships, nor do we have the ability to force them to materialize. We are not in control of when we meet our future partners. I don't say that to discourage you. I say it to help you feel more free.

Finding someone is never going to be more important than your well-being, feelings, safety, and sanity. Ever. I wish the dating space wasn't what it is, but it is. And it isn't serving those of us who are looking for real, respectful, lasting love. You deserve everything you want, and I believe you'll have it. If the dating space isn't giving you anything but disappointment, frustration, and hopelessness, then get out—you're allowed to. You are as free as you have ever been, and will ever be, to put yourself first. You are more important than "finding someone," and you always were.

8

Earning It

One of the hardest parts of being single can often be how little sense it makes. Things that happen to us in singlehood, or maybe more specifically in dating, rarely follow logic. Instead of letting go and understanding that the dating space can be illogical, we tend to feel crazy ourselves instead. You're not crazy. Sometimes, this shit just doesn't add up. You're not unworthy of love. You're not unattractive to your future partners. You're not any of the flaws society and our brains love to attach to singlehood. What you actually are is brave enough to face the world every day and to want to be loved within it. You're not insane—you're a hero.

Have you ever felt like you've "put in the work" to stop being single? Have you ever thought, "I've tried so hard, for so long—shouldn't they be here by now"? Have you ever felt an imbalance in the amount of effort you've put into dating versus the results you've actually seen from that effort? That's because—I'll say it again—dating is one area of life where effort doesn't have to match reward. It's also because there's no amount of suffering we can endure in the dating space that ever has to "earn" us a partner.

There is a false narrative around "earning" partnership that we need to reframe. Simply stated, you cannot suffer so much in the dating space that you'll finally be rewarded with the love of your life. Difficult dating experiences do not go into some sort of bank that lets you cash out a partner after a certain amount of difficulty. That isn't a thing.

I'd really like single women to shed the notion that they have to put up with hell in order to earn a spouse. You don't. Think of all the married and partnered people you know. Did they have to crawl across a field of flaming barbed wire first? Or did they just kind of...meet someone?

In my opinion, we equate suffering through dating with earning partnership because we've exalted romantic love to such heights that *of course* we have to "earn it" first. How could we ever just effortlessly find something so wonderful? That's not how life works! Life is suffering! Beauty is pain! And then we just accept a toxic dating culture because we're expecting one. We're expecting finding love to be hard because something as *amazing* as romantic love certainly must come at a price.

This theory applies in plenty of other scenarios. Do you remember all those shitty internships where you thought you had to grovel professionally and pick up salads for people in order to "pay your dues"? You didn't. Every internship should have actually been teaching us to do the work we had an interest in, because that's where we were choosing to spend our time as valid human beings. We weren't lesser-status humans; we were young people in need of experience and education. Any nonsense menial labor was just people senior to us feeling the gratification of making someone below them do the shit they once had to do for someone else. If you have an intern now, make sure they're learning something, cool?

Workplace reframing is its own book, but here, let's focus our efforts on singlehood and "finding love," a phrase that only belongs in nineties-era romantic movies where someone always owns a lake house. Let's explore the garbage notion that you can somehow suffer your way out of singlehood.

Take my hand and walk with me down this mental pathway:

1. I don't want to be single.
2. I should date so I won't be single anymore.
3. Holy shit, dating is a nightmare.
4. Not dating feels like I'm not doing enough.
5. Maybe I should try more dating.
6. Oh, god, it really is a nightmare.
7. Why does dating have to be this bad?
8. Mommy!
9. I don't understand why this is so hard. Everyone else is finding someone—why can't I find someone?

10. Haven't I suffered enough already?
11. I don't want to be single.

How many times do you think you've run through a mental cycle like this one during your singlehood? I did it more times than I can count, and it made me more miserable than I want to remember.

There was simply no logic in it. In ten years—*ten fucking years*—of dating, I never once had a partner result from my effort. Not only that, I had an overwhelming number of bad experiences in the dating world as well. It wasn't just that I wasn't finding my partner; I was also absorbing *so much negativity* on a road to nowhere. The experiences add up over time, and we always assume there will be some sweet release at the end, when we finally meet our partners. This assumption isn't necessarily false, because you may very well meet your partner at some point. Or not. I don't know, and I can't tell you. It's the fact that we can't know what will help us let go of our old beliefs about earning it, because we can't earn it. I hope this reality inspires an evaluation of how we're spending our single time.

It doesn't have to be ten years for you. Any amount of suffering through singlehood misery and a cruel dating culture is too long in my opinion. But our shame and hatred of singlehood, combined with our fear of being alone forever, add up to continuing to suffer, voluntarily. We think doing so will earn us a partner one day, but in this *Alice in Wonderland* dating culture we live in, dating can get away with never giving you a damn thing.

Remember that punishment can't fix something you never did wrong. For our purposes, I'm speaking of self-punishment that single people keep partaking in, on the assumption that all this swiping, messaging, dating, and the aftermath will all add up to something eventually. We think we can earn a relationship by suffering "enough" in dating, so we put up with the punishment of a broken dating culture, thinking it will earn us love.

But if we always deserved love from the beginning, what is the point of punishment?

We need to talk about turns. I hear single women asking themselves, and sometimes directly asking me, "When is it my turn? Shouldn't it be my turn by now? I've tried everything, I've done everything, I can't stop wanting it to be my turn!"

Lovelies, there are no turns. Your entire life is "your turn." There are no guarantees in dating and partnership, ever. There's no order, or sense, or turns, and that's okay. It's okay to let go and accept we're not in charge here—and to accept we're not paying for a future partnership by suffering right now. Stop waiting for it to be your "turn" for a partner, and start recognizing it's already your turn to live a valid, full, happy life. A partner isn't required for that, but one's still allowed to show up all the same.

A word on "chances," too, because I often hear how women who walk away from a dating space that makes them miserable feel like they're not "doing enough" to find someone and end their singleness. They feel like by not putting active effort into dating, they're "lowering their chances."

In my opinion, we don't have to *do* anything, because being single is not a plague we have to cure, but I'll humor us here. I have the same "chances" of meeting someone without actively dating as I did while I *was* dating, as proven by the fact that dating never delivered anything resembling a relationship to me. How could I be lowering my chances if all the chances I gave to dating added up to nothing anyway? Wait, it wasn't nothing—dating actually amounted to negative, disappointing, punishing experiences. So really, I've lowered my chances of all *that* shit happening, instead.

We're so reluctant to walk away from a dating world that doesn't treat us well, because we're somehow convinced he's just one swipe away. I one-swipe-awayed half my adulthood. I thought *surely*, all this suffering must lead to something, right? It never did, and instead of giving it ten more years of chances to "work," I am simply done placing myself in the line of dating fire. That doesn't mean I'm "lowering my chances." It means I am living my life.

There's no "giving up" in this. I think just the opposite, actually. I think I'm finally entertaining the possibility that my future partnerships don't have to involve suffering first. I'm acknowledging I'm worthy of love, right now. Not after I've suffered, not after I've "worked on myself," right *now*. Not suffering through dating anymore isn't the same thing as giving up on love entirely.

I have no doubt that my future partner(s) and I are meant to meet. I do not believe I was put on this earth to live the entirety of my life without romantic relationships. That doesn't make logical sense to me. Romantic love is something I want, and I know I deserve to have it, because I'm here. I'm a person, valid and worthy, and people fall in love *all the damn time*. Knowing all this, I can trust he and I will find some other way to meet that doesn't involve a massive struggle on my part. Dating apps and dating culture no longer have access to me. They weren't respecting that access, so I removed it. Instead of forcing myself onto just one path to partnership that was hurting me, I opened myself up to literally all the other ones imaginable, and they don't hurt a bit.

I used to think all the years that I'd been single were going to add up to an amazing future partner. Old thought patterns told me if I'd been single for this long, with this much difficulty, in the end the partner I'd receive would be worth it. He'd be worth what I went through. Now I know that it doesn't work that way. My single years aren't the time I spent earning a partner. They're the time I spent discovering my purpose, worth, and values. I wasn't being punished with years of difficult singledom; I was being gifted with time and space to become who I was meant to be.

When uncomfortable, unpleasant, opposite-of-what-we-wanted things happen to us in the dating space, no one's keeping score of how many times we're hurt or unhappy. We're playing this game under the false assumption that everyone is playing fair. Modern dating culture is never playing fair, and it's certainly not on your team. It doesn't have your best interests at heart because your best interests hurt its profits. Remember what I said about paying for maybes. The last thing a dating app wants you to do is stop using it because you actually found someone.

We cling to "success stories." The friend you have who opened her dating app to delete it and saw a message from the man who became her husband a year later. The cousin who met her spouse on her second-ever app date. The coworker who Zoomed with someone for a month and eventually moved in with her new boyfriend during a fucking pandemic. We love these stories, because we see them as "proof" that dating works.

The thing is, it worked for someone else. In a world that doesn't abide by rules, it never has to work out for you the same way. And you don't have to give it endless chances to, thinking that eventually it will be your turn. You get to have more agency over your life than that.

I never say these things to devastate us, only to give us hope—a kind of hope that I think we're ignoring. We're so deep in the muck of dating, hoping we'll meet someone in exchange for all our effort, that we've forgotten how to hope we'll meet someone *any other way*. For every story of two people who met through dating apps or even IRL dating, there are so many stories of people who met by chance. The fact that things can happen in any way imaginable gives me *so much more hope* than I had when I thought the only way I'd ever meet someone was by swiping into infinity or constantly asking friends if they "know anybody for me."

If meeting a partner is based on chance, we're free. We're free to live our lives as single people without the chore of dating permanently on our to-do list. We don't have to focus so much of our attention on "finding someone" when there's nothing we can do, and no amount we can suffer, to make it happen. We can let go, and let it happen—or better still, let go and stop needing it to.

When you're happily single, you stop thinking about when it's going to be "your turn." That nagging feeling just goes away, and you live freely. You start to see singlehood as a beautiful time, and only those who truly add something wonderful to your life are worth leaving singlehood for. It's possible to pull your head out of your app and start seeing all the freedom and possibilities single life affords you—for however long you have it.

There's a different way to view everything we've been through in the single and dating spaces. We don't have to view it as suffering. We can choose to view our experiences as education, strengthening, and growth. Reflecting on my darkest single days, the ones I spent swiping until my thumb ached, was once really hard for me to do. It was so painful and shameful, and for a long time, that's all I thought it would ever be. But when I look back on it through a lens of education, I am grateful. I've let go of hating those times. I've started appreciating them for everything they taught me, and my heart feels less heavy as a result.

You don't need permission to let go. You don't need special training or courses. You can reframe it all, for free, right now. You can choose to change the way you think about singlehood and dating, and therefore change the way you feel. It was difficult, and that will always be true. It was painful, and your pain will always be valid. But you're allowed to reframe it all to see how it got you here, to learn the value and lessons it gave you—that's a possibility, too.

> Old thought: *There must be a great partner waiting for me at the end of all this suffering, right?*
>
> New thought: *I can't buy my partner by suffering through the worst of dating, as proven by the fact that I haven't yet. Exactly how much do I think I have to go through in order to have partnership? Why do I think I deserve to suffer more than others who found partnership more easily? Maybe I don't have to participate in the worst of dating. This isn't a transaction—it's life. I'm allowed to live it in a way that's best for me and my well-being. If dating isn't respecting my well-being, I don't have to do it. Dating isn't payment for a future partner.*

I spent ten years in dating culture, and then I let go. I cleared my head of the ever-present "search mode" that I'd let nestle there for so long. I stopped waiting for something to "work," and I let go of it needing to be my "turn." I acknowledged that I wasn't alive simply to search for someone else, and I released the need for someone else to love me in order to feel valid in the world. I reconnected with my joy, optimism, and well-being in exchange.

Your turn.

9

In Comparison

I'll just say it: other people's happiness is hard to swallow, especially when you feel like you don't have any of your own. We're living in a time when there's more access to other people's happiness—I mean social media posts—so naturally, as singles we might sometimes feel the sting of being a have-not.

I mean honestly, fifty years ago, if your high school boyfriend got engaged seven states away from where you are now, you'd probably never know about it. These days, however, we almost *have* to know when things happen to other people, because if a happy moment falls in a forest, no one can give it a "like." So they post, we see, we compare, we cry. I've done it. You've done it. It's okay. Let's talk about why it's happening and what we can do to feel better.

I'm not confused about why IRL comparison and social media stalking happen, or why they hurt so badly. Singles have centered and prized romantic love and couplehood (actually, everyone has). So when other people get those things and we don't, *and* we have to watch, the sting is *potent*. I know why this is happening, but I don't know why it never dawns on us earlier to stop. It took me ten years, and I've heard of slow learners, but my goodness.

Comparison isn't helping anybody, and it's certainly not helping singles. We have a bad habit of seeing and hearing about what other people have and then viewing these relationships and life milestones as mirrors of what we *don't* have—but remember, this is a choice. We can choose to see things as proof of what's possible instead. Why is it always "Why does she have it and I don't?" and never "She got it, and I'm just as human and worthy as she is; therefore, that can happen to me, too?" Singleness isn't an implied negative unless you choose to see it as one.

Remember to have patience with yourself as you're choosing new thoughts, and treat yourself kindly. It's okay if this takes time and practice. We're working with *years* of old beliefs here—I promise you're doing better than you think.

Simple shifts that reframe what's actually happening can genuinely improve our feelings about singlehood. We're simply taking the thing that's happening and viewing it from the other side. Someone else met someone, got engaged, etc., and we can choose to see it through a lens of possibility, rather than one of lack. That's an option for us. I don't see comparison doing single women any favors, but

I *have* seen a benefit in swapping comparison for new perspectives. With practice, reframing can help singles stop comparing and create a real shift in how we feel.

When we're stuck in a comparison hole, in addition to just filling our lives with incoming jealousy fodder, we're also ignoring so much good that's going on with us right now. It's hard to see what's in front of you when you only ever pay attention to what's in front of other people. It's also hard when you think what's happening to other people is more valid than what's happening to you.

Comparison also denies us uniqueness. It denies us the possibility that maybe our lives were never meant to look like the lives we envy. Have you ever explored precisely *why* you want those engagements and relationships and infinity pool vacations with awkward sunset poses? What do you think it's like to have them? Exactly how *outstanding* have we built this stuff up to be in our minds? Relationships don't cure you of a deadly disease. They just let you split rent and movie snacks—let's calm down. (I'm not degrading the value of love, I'm just trying to offer a little balance—it's fine.)

Social media has become a space where the people posting seek validation, and the people watching expose themselves to a shitload of jealousy fodder. I'm not saying social media is the only place that triggers our envy and jealousy—but it's a pretty damn big one, don't you think? When was the last time you felt bad because something good happened to someone who wasn't you? I'd bet green money you were looking at your phone.

Comparison can certainly happen IRL, too—from big moments like weddings and bridal showers to smaller, everyday triggers like a couple holding hands while walking down the sidewalk so that you have to walk in the *street* in order to pass the snail's pace at which they're ambling. *Side note*: nothing shits in my sandbox like a slow walker—nothing.

It's important to understand these events are not in charge of you. You are not simply a plaything to be tossed around by other people's lives. You're here for a whole lot more than that, and I believe shedding a comparison habit will help you see it.

I want to break comparison down into what it really communicates to us. What happens when we look at what someone else has and instantly feel bad because we don't have it, too? Do we want what they have, or do we want something of our own? While it's 100 percent okay to want something of our own, why does seeing things other people have in their romantic lives have the capacity to make us feel *so bad*? Does that seem fair or balanced to you? I want you to know it's genuinely possible to stop comparing—and to feel much better. We're going to walk through a few realities of comparison that I think will help you reframe it for yourself. They certainly helped me.

First, timelines. We are all on our own unique, tailor-made timelines that become the one-of-a-kind story of our lives. This isn't a widely celebrated truth. Instead, we're pretty much fed one societally kosher life timeline, and if we can't squeeze ourselves into it, we're shamed: college, job, date, partner, marry, house, baby, second baby, send babies to college, and so on and so forth until the end of humanity because we ruined our climate. And by the way, more than half of that timeline needs to happen in your twenties, or you're late—sorry sweetie.

My life story didn't fit into the narrow window afforded me by societally accepted standards, and I'm not even halfway to my life expectancy yet. These days, I'm *grateful* I didn't follow this path, but I'm also sorry we're fed standards and timelines that are too narrow to include everybody—or to include any sort of variety. Personally, when I look at the traditional life timeline, I don't see goals; I see boredom. Yeah, I said it.

I'm sorry that sometimes our unique or "unconventional" (what an annoying word) timelines are shamed, but I hope it comforts you to know that those shaming you aren't actually living your life, and therefore, their opinions don't matter. Just because someone shames your life doesn't mean their shame is true, and it doesn't mean their shame has to become yours.

Instead of one decade—your twenties—being prized, awesome, and accepted, I wish many, many more decades were included in that narrative. Instead, we start making people feel "old" on their thirtieth birthday. Isn't that wild? I'm sorry, but I refuse to consider only one-third or so of my life as "the good part." What am I supposed to tell myself for the next five or six *decades*? That I'm *over*? Absolutely not.

The dumbest decade of my life was never meant to determine so much of the rest of my future. I think societally accepted timelines are a little irresponsible. I was nowhere near emotionally mature or wise enough to get married before I was thirty. I cannot imagine how dependent I would have been on my relationship to make me feel real, worthy, and loved. There was a different timeline waiting for me, one that involved learning by experience, developing a strong sense of self and value, and hopefully translating those things into helping other people. You wouldn't be reading this book right now if I'd gotten married in 2011. Not for nothing, I'd rather have the book.

The woman I am now knows she wants a relationship because she *wants* one—not because she *needs* one, and twenty-nine-year-old me didn't know the damn difference. My singlehood at thirty-nine isn't me being a failure or "late;" it's me dodging a bullet. Maybe several of them.

The notion of other people "finding love" sooner than I did and therefore being somehow better people than me is laughable. How can someone's life speed make them more lovable or valid than me? *Hurry up, Shani, better get married exactly when everyone else does or you'll be weird!* First of fucking all, I like my weirdness. Second, I'd rather be weird and on a timeline that's made just for me than married along with the herd for the sake of fitting in. Fitting in is overvalued, and I've never seen much good come from doing something "because everyone else was doing it." Have you?

I'm sorry other people finding things before us can feel so bad. I know that feeling, and I remember hating it, too.

Honestly, I was opening Instagram to see cute dog photos, not to be emotionally crushed by someone's Thanksgiving engagement, Jesus.

Which brings me to my next comparison point: someone else's happiness doesn't have anything to do with you. When we have negative reactions to other people's happiness, we're inserting ourselves into their story. We're letting their story say something about us, even though we're not in that story in the first place. Someone else partnering, getting engaged, getting married, buying a house together—none of these things are a reflection on what we don't have unless we allow them to be. What they actually are is a reflection of our feelings about our own singlehood, and that, my friends, is a perfect opportunity for reframing.

One of the ways single women like to numb the pain of comparison is by imagining the smiling couple in the photo is actually miserable in real life. We love to assume the photo is super fabricated and posed and that it's hiding some dark truth about how bad the relationship *really* is. We love to assume they've literally paused a huge fight just to take a photo.

Understand something: couples don't have to be miserable for single people to be happy. Other people's happiness isn't an affront to those who are single. Other people's happiness has nothing to do with us *at all*.

Love and happiness aren't in limited supply. They aren't stolen from us every time someone else finds them. One person acquiring some happiness doesn't rob from the stash available to you. You can look at something happening to someone else that you would also like to happen to you and understand that you haven't lost anything.

Let's please also shed the notion that "there are no good ones left." I truly can't. When last I googled, Earth's population was 7.6 billion. Yet, somehow, we think there's "nobody left" for us? That sounds like a swiping problem to me. Stop getting stuck head-down in five different dating apps that have all the same people on them, and remember you live on a whole-ass planet. It's also a little self-centered! Literally 7.6 billion people on Earth, and you think *you're* the one that the Universe has decided to withhold all partnership options from? Yes, I serve my tea boiling, what of it?

Honestly, you don't want the couples you see on social media and out in the world to be miserable. There's flawed logic in that. If you want to be in a couple but think all the couples you see are secretly miserable, what does that say about the thing you want? I genuinely hope the couples I see are happy, because I intend to be one of them someday, when it's the right time and the right person for me. Secret sinister couplehood unhappiness thoughts are not the right look.

You've probably heard the Theodore Roosevelt quote, "Comparison is the thief of joy." I actually think comparison steals much more. It can come out of nowhere and rob you of a good mood, a productive day, an empowered mindset—and comparison isn't entitled to have that much sway over you. We really don't need things that happen to other people somewhere else influencing what's happening to us right here and now.

I have an exercise for us. It's a trick I use to help me when I feel triggered by a case of the "why don't I have thats." Instead of running through whatever frustrated, angry, and jealous self-talk I might have launched into before, I do this:

Old thought: *Why her and not me?*
New thought: *I'm so happy for them.*

That's it! It's really simple. *"I'm so happy for them."* Every time you see a couple kissing on a park bench, or picking out a sofa at Ikea, or getting engaged at Disneyland: "I'm so happy for them." What we're doing here is training your jealousy reflex to become a joy reflex instead.

Cheesy? Kind of! Effective? With some practice, you betcha! Try this simple change of thought until it becomes your instinct. Start looking at the things you want happening to other people with joy, as reminders of what's possible, rather than as little daggers in your heart every time. You might have to employ a bit of "fake it till you make it," but honestly, not much! Feelings with some buoyancy to them are always easier to attach to than feelings that drag us down. I think you're going to prefer "I'm so happy for them" feelings to "Why isn't this happening to me?" feelings, and fast.

Have you ever thought about how comparison steals your genuine happiness for other people? I am so sick of looking at my phone and scowling—that's not the person I want to be. I want to be happy for other people's happiness. That is a core value of mine, and the way the world has taught me to hate singlehood doesn't get to rob me of who I want to be. Similarly, I never want to be super happy when someone breaks up or gets divorced (unless they're super happy for themselves!). That's not the kind of person I can be proud of, someone who thrives when others feel down. That's not the mood I want for my life.

There are a few other little practices you can try when comparison seems particularly potent:

If someone else is a dentist, do you ever ask yourself why you're not also a dentist? If someone loves white chocolate (I don't know why they would, but stay with me), do you ask yourself why you can't have the same taste in confections? If someone is good at soccer, do you envy their talent? Maybe! Do you let that envy ruin your mood or your day, or is it just something true that doesn't have to impact you because it has nothing to do with you?

We've over-prioritized romantic love and relationships, friends. Nothing sparks envy like they do, and we need to think about that. If we spend all our time looking at other people's lives as nothing more than reflections of what we don't have, we'll be exhausted and miserable. We can choose not to compare, and we can reframe comparison for ourselves until not comparing becomes the norm. I'm not saying it will work every time, but we can train the jealousy out of ourselves, and replace it with proof of what's possible and a warmth for other people's joy. That's how I'd rather live.

Life is allowed to be tailored to us, and customized to what will bring out the best in our future. Do you really want to alter that because someone met their partner faster than you did? Or is there room for a little more letting go and trusting that you're not here to do things the way everyone else is doing them? Why can't that be a good thing, rather than a jealousy-inducing thing?

I know it's hard to see people in love when you want to be in love. I understand this deeply, and I lived with that kind of pain for a long, long time. I will never invalidate you or your desire for love and partnership—just the opposite. I want love and partnership for you and for myself. But I'm also acknowledging it's not always going to happen for us when or how we want it to, or how it's happened for other people. I don't see that as a bad thing anymore. I see it as life being customized to me, and bespoke is always better. It's possible for things to happen in a way we don't want them to and for us to be okay anyway.

I never mean this reframing of singlehood to relieve you of your wants and desires. Keep them! I think they're beautiful and valid because they're yours. This process is more about improving the way you manage the day-to-day feelings of singlehood. Remember: we can feel good about our singlehood and remain open to relationships at the same time—that's allowed.

Singlehood has been painted as a plague for far too long, and I think it deserves to be seen as a gift. I never got married before I was meant to. I've had thirteen years to grow and learn about myself and the person I want to become, without accommodating another person in my life and home at the same time. I've learned what I like and don't like, and I've learned how I want to feel in my romantic relationships before I begin them, rather than having to adjust them after the fact. I have the perspective of someone who has had time to herself. The gifts are really endless when you start to add them up.

Time isn't something we're losing every day that we're not meeting someone. It's time we've been gifted to spend any way we like. Our homes are not void of another person; they're full of *us* and all the ways we love to nest and dwell. Our hearts are not empty of love; they have the opportunity to love in all the ways people can love, not *only* in the romantic way—friends, family, pets, places, hobbies, work, adventures. There is no lack of love for us, but comparison will trick you into seeing nothing but emptiness. Don't let it.

1 0

Scared Away

Single life can feel like a million things. We can feel desire, longing, loneliness, hope, fear, freedom, exhaustion, rage, optimism, pessimism, lunacy, everything. All the emotions are valid, and entirely understandable—this shit's not easy. But there's one feeling that brings me sorrow for single women more than any other: it's when we feel inauthentic.

Nothing puts hair in my lip gloss like single life stealing our authenticity—when it takes away who we are and replaces us with someone else, someone who thinks they have to change themselves and their feelings or restrict their actions in order to be loved. We've let modern single life tell us we have to alter who we naturally are if we ever want to find and keep a partner, and I don't have to stay silent about that.

Have you ever stopped yourself from saying something you wanted to say? Stopped yourself from sending a text you wanted to send? Have you had the instinct to hold someone's hand or give someone an unsolicited kiss but thought it would be better not to? Has dating ever felt like you were playing one very large and elaborate game of Operation from when we were kids? As if you're tweezing into your time with someone, careful not to touch an electrified edge? That's what I mean by being inauthentic. Inauthenticity feels like you're dating on eggshells.

If you've experienced this, you've probably been doing *a lot* in the name of not "scaring them away." You've been afraid that any and everything you do in the dating space will result in whomever you're interested in skittering away like a frightened gerbil. This dynamic puts someone else in a place of power, while you're belittled into overthinking every idea and action that occurs to you because...*what if it scares them away?*

I say scare that motherfucker, but let's get into something a little more elegant and nuanced, shall we?

Simply stated, you are not always doing something wrong by simply existing in ways that come naturally to you. I understand what it's like to always feel like you're doing it wrong. Or maybe you look wrong, or you act wrong, or somehow you're not—at all times—attracting potential partners by every possible means available to you as a human woman.

The negative, false, and outdated narratives around singlehood have real-life consequences. Single women live through experiences every day that many people will never see and probably never understand. Most people, certainly coupled people, don't walk around in fear that everything they do, every quality about them, has the potential to scare away someone who might help them escape singlehood. This is an exhausting way to live, and we're living it privately.

Not everyone knows what it's like to be afraid every text you send is the last text someone else will ever bother to respond to. Societally, we make fun of women changing their outfits fifteen times before a date, but single women know what it's like to actually think what you're wearing can impact your fucking future. This stuff is real—it's really happening to us. I know what it's like to live in fear that you're scaring people away, and I see you.

I remember going on a great date once. I had awesome banter with this guy, we got along really well, and it was simply a nice night out. Something happened the next day that reminded me of something we'd both found funny during the date. I texted to tell him about it. He was annoyed that my text had woken him up (it was eleven o'clock in the morning), and I never heard from him again. I take a lot of pleasure in the fact that I don't remember his name or what he looked like. He was scared away, and I'm happy about it. I would never want to be in a relationship with someone capable of dismissing me with the ease that he did. But dating culture has trained single women to believe *I* was actually wrong for texting him after the date first.

I should have waited (heaven knows how long) for him to text me, and then maybe I'd still be dating that dipshit to this day. The right person for me will be genuinely happy to hear from me, whenever it occurs to me to text. He probably also won't sleep past 11 a.m. on a perfectly good Saturday.

The right people for you will never be "scared away" by who you actually are. Authenticity in dating is undervalued. Instead, single women receive message after message that we should change something, do something differently, and *then* we'll attract someone to us—*then* they will spend more time with us and fall in love with us and we'll be happy forevermore. Love doesn't work that way. There is no magic change you can make, one flaw you can fix, one text you can avoid sending, that will make the right partner for you show up—or stay. Who you authentically are draws people to you. But our modern dating culture doesn't really encourage our authenticity, and I'm sorry this is what's become of single-hood and dating. Let's reframe it, shall we?

I know what it's like to live in constant fear you're scaring someone away. I also know it's possible to stop giving a shit. Even better, it's possible to start seeing "scaring them away" as a damn good thing.

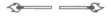

The dating world is full of those eggshells I mentioned earlier, or as you know them, lies we tell other people in order to be accepted. We live in a dating culture built atop a tower of eggshells, and we don't know where the hell to put our feet. Single women take in a lot of messaging, from society but also just from shitbirds on dating apps, that we have to approach something that matters to us like it doesn't matter at all, or else run the risk of scaring people away. Dating culture tells us if we don't lie, we won't win.

A word on being "chill." Relaxed. Cool. Loosey-goosey. Because that's what we're supposed to be, right? We're supposed to take our genuine desires for love and companionship and twist them into something inauthentic that matches the male preference to keep one's options open. Dating culture has trained us to see ourselves as options in a sea of options. So when we meet someone, we're cognizant that we're just one of the endless women for him to choose from. We'd better not do anything to scare him away! You know, things like expecting the bare minimum manners, reciprocity, respect, interest, attention, anything really. It's better not to ask *anything* of players in the dating space, because there's probably someone else out there who will ask even less. I bet he'll like her more.

Does that feel authentic to you? Do you want to want nothing from the men you date just in case your entirely valid expectations of someone scare him away? Does that even feel like dating to you?

You don't have to be chill if you're not chill. Dating culture will ask single women to lie to themselves and others in many different ways, but chillness is one of the most prevalent. Our society treats finding love and lifelong (sure) partnership as literally the most celebration-worthy thing a woman can do, but as far as searching for that thing goes, she'd better pretend like she couldn't care less. Otherwise, she runs the risk of not being "chill" enough for guys to like her. If she isn't "chill" about things, she'll scare him away.

There is something so archaic about asking a woman to be aloof, to perform a quiet cabaret for potential partners that communicates how disinterested she is, no matter how interested she actually happens to be in either one particular person or partnership itself. The gamification of attracting a man is exhausting, and quite frankly not met with a matched level of effort on the other side often enough. If we have to be stressed out about this, then by god so do they. It's as if the common heterosexual male finds the notion of...I don't fucking know, conversation, interaction, affection, and access to another human being simply too much for his delicate sensibilities.

Single women are allowed to give a damn about dating. We're allowed to give a damn about finding love. Being open to possibility, and the vulnerability that requires in today's dating culture, doesn't make us annoying—it makes us brave. I'm furious with dating culture for making single women feel wrong for having hopes for their own futures. And I'm furious with dating culture for dashing those hopes again, and again, and again, and again without ever having to answer for it.

The prioritization of chillness has made single women think that we're "too much" just by being anything at all. It asks us to adopt a relaxed attitude toward something we may not find very relaxing. It also puts us in competition with one other, which is gross. When we're asked to "feel less" than we naturally feel, we end up walking through life perpetually feeling wrong. We feel wrong for feeling anything. *Y'all.*

I have no chill. But instead of the "Why isn't he *textiiiinnngg meeeeee?*" brunch wail, my no chill involves having very little patience for bullshit. If the level of interest I'm feeling and displaying for another person isn't reciprocated, I cut that person off immediately. My level of stick around is set to zero, so he needs to do something to earn my attention, just like I make an effort to earn his, or auf Wiedersehen.

It's a reclaiming. Instead of minimizing my own feelings down to nothing, lest I scare away a potential partner, I'm centering them and the respect and reciprocity I know I deserve. It feels a hell of a lot better to center *me* and what I actually want than to ignore my authenticity for the sake of finding a relationship by any means. Singlehood doesn't suck enough for me to turn into someone I'm not.

I acknowledge that my natural feelings and way of operating in the romantic world cannot possibly be wrong—not for the people who are right for me. For everyone else who *isn't* right for me, they're a brilliant filter. If who I authentically am is too much for you, then leave, and leave quickly. Save us both some time.

I *have to* feel my feelings and show them, or I might attract the wrong people. Attracting the wrong people is what scares me, not the idea of some dude dashing away like a threatened insect if I dare to do so much as text him, "Hi, how are you?"

A common scenario I see in my work is women finding themselves in situations where they want more to happen, but more isn't happening. For example, getting "stuck" in texting-only exchanges with men that never materialize into dates in person, because the men they're texting never bring it up. A single woman in this situation might be scared to insist upon meeting in person and taking things forward, because what if that scares away the guy she's texting and she never hears from him again?

Here's whatcha do when this happens: stop fucking texting. You are never stuck. You are making a choice. You are choosing to continue responding to texts, and you are choosing not to suggest that the two of you take things out into the real world by meeting up. If he's not making plans with you when you've asked for that, stop texting him. If you feel scared to ask for what you actually want, stop texting him. Your hesitancy is a sign you can learn to listen to. It means he isn't making you feel like you're in a secure place when you communicate with him. You're allowed to take this feeling as an indicator that you should move on.

I don't say these things to blame single women for the scenarios we find ourselves in. I say them to remind us all we have choices, and we are allowed to exercise those choices. Sometimes we don't just say, "Hey, let's meet up," because we think doing so will scare him away. Dating isn't just happening to you. You are allowed to happen to dating right back.

If all that's ever happened between you and someone else are text messages, they can't be scared away, because they were never really there. It's okay to acknowledge something is happening to you in the dating space that you don't like. When you feel stuck, understand you do not have to wait for the other person's behavior to change—you can change yours. That is allowed, and if it "scares them away," good.

Do you even want someone who can be scared away by suggesting you do something beyond texting each other? Does that sound like someone you genuinely want? Or is it just that you have an "iron in the fire" and anything at all feels better than nothing? I have a secret: letting go of people you're afraid to scare away isn't nothing. It's reclaiming your time and authenticity. It feels a hell of a lot better than dating on eggshells.

The two outcomes of saying something you authentically want to say are either the person you're talking to agrees, and something you want to happen, happens—or this person gets scared away, and you've just avoided spending any more time and energy on someone who never had any intention of giving you what you want. You've lost nothing. By taking the action you're afraid will scare someone away, you actually lose nothing.

If they can be scared away, they were meant to be scared away. The actions that come naturally to you will not scare away the people who are right for you. Otherwise, you'd have to act unnaturally forever. Send the text, hold the hand, find out the next time you're going to see each other, if that's what you want to know. Who you authentically are will not be scary to someone you should be spending time with; it will be the very thing that draws them closer.

I don't believe we're born with a drive to minimize ourselves. I think we learn to take or avoid actions in the name of not scaring people away. We come by these behaviors honestly, and I want us all to be kind to ourselves and forgive ourselves for taking part in them—especially while we're working on developing new thoughts and habits. If you struggle with self-kindness and/or habit change, I encourage you to look into the work of Shahroo Izadi.

We've been groomed to be ashamed of our singlehood, because the world sees single women as sad, unfinished, flawed beings. And honestly, to this day, I've never really gotten to the root of why. Maybe people in pairs make society more comfortable. Maybe we've built our world around things made for two. Or maybe a single woman on her own is simply having too good of a time.

It always feels like it's on us, the women in heterosexual dating culture, to bear the burden of dating itself. It's always the woman who is expected to "work on herself" or seek out dating advice in order not to be single anymore. Or it's single women who are "high maintenance" or "too much," rather than the single men in the dating space ever getting called out as not being enough. Who do we assume needs to change more often in the dating space, single women or single men? If we're going to ask people to alter who they are in order to find love, doesn't that suggest we'd impose upon everyone equally? Nah. The assumption is *women*

have to change, become more chill, or expect less, in order to meet men at the lower level of effort they're willing to put forth. Yes, I said it, and I'd say it again. Single men haven't *ever* given a shit about my feelings, so I couldn't care less about theirs right now. It's *always* single women who have to change to fit dating, rather than dating ever needing to change to fit single women. Personally, I think this is fucked.

A lot of reframing singlehood has to do with reclaiming our driver's seat. It isn't always about what *someone else* likes or what's going to scare *someone else* away. We can, maybe without realizing it, get in the habit of prioritizing other people in our singlehood and dating experiences, and we don't have to do that. We matter, too. We have agency over what's happening, too. The narrative of a single woman waiting to be chosen by a man is a dead one. Deceased. This isn't about being chosen, and honestly, I don't even think it's about us choosing, either. I think relationships are about two people coming together on equal footing and deciding to spend time together as they move through life. My point is, the other person is not in charge. They are not selecting you from a lineup. You don't need to dazzle, please, or entice them without actually asking anything real of them, lest they be scared away. Everything is not up to them—it's up to how *you* want things to go, too.

Get out of the passenger seat of dating and singlehood, and remember you know how to drive. We are not resigned to a life of expecting and asking less. They are also responsible for delivering more, or getting the fuck out of your way.

We've been taught to really, *really* enjoy and prioritize having that "iron in the fire." The absence of "something going on" in our romantic lives can make singles feel very lacking, lazy, impatient, or some combination of all three. We hang a lot of hopes on irons in the fire, and we tend to do anything and everything to keep them there. Because I haven't used enough analogies yet, it's like you've "got one on the hook," and it's a very exciting, determined moment for you. You want to reel in whatever's at the end of the fishing pole, and you're scared one false move will snap the line. Except in this case, a "false move" is anything totally normal that dating culture has told you is "too much."

Therefore, when something happens and we do scare someone away, or it fizzles out for some other reason, we can be *very* disappointed, sad, even depressed—regardless of how much or little we'd invested in the situation and often regardless of how much we actually liked them. We give up the driver's seat and let someone else decide whether or not a relationship moves forward, and how. Where are *we* in these scenarios? What decisions are *we* making?

The importance we've placed on relationships and the grind of dating culture can also make us forget there's more out there in the world than one person who isn't really showing up for us. Every person you meet is not the last person you will ever meet. You do not need to hold on to every potential partner no matter how disappointing they are because you're worried another one will never come along.

Stop fearing the fucking future. Okay that felt harsh, but I do mean it. I'll talk about this more and explain *how* to stop fearing the future in a later chapter (it's about not settling—you'll love it). For now, remember there are 7.6 *billion* people on Earth last time demographers made an educated guess, and you are alive and going about your business on a highly populated planet. It's illogical to think you'll never come into contact with more potential partners—unless you lock yourself in a bunker of some kind for the rest of your life.

Any dismissal of logic is just our old, negative singlehood narratives that love to tell us being single is bad, while also telling us we'll never be in a relationship again, because the very fact we're still single makes us the worst person ever, and so on and so forth until you lose your marbles. Sure, relationships are great, but have you ever tried shedding old singlehood narratives and not letting them influence the way you feel about yourself and your value? Have you ever tried a little logic? It's the *best*.

You can even take it deeper. The person you desire right now is not the last person you will ever desire. The person who desires *you* is not the last person capable of such a thing. We've learned to live in a scarcity mentality and to treat every potential romantic relationship like it's the last one that will ever come along. We believe there are "no good ones left" because we're too old, or we live in too small a place—or whatever reasons our brains find that make it easier to stay in mental maelstroms of shame and punishment instead of entertaining the idea we don't have to constantly look for someone and we don't have to fear that enjoying singlehood means we'll be single forever. Do you see how these themes keep coming up? That's because this bullshit really does impact our day-to-day single lives and can cause us to feel like we're on an endless treadmill of husband-hunting. By similar logic, letting go of these old narratives and reframing them can improve our lives and help us feel significantly better, more valid, and more... you know, chill.

We've been taught to center the pursuit of a relationship. Nothing is supposed to be more important to a single woman than that. My worry is that we're centering "making it work" and avoiding "scaring them away" instead of our own thoughts and feelings about others and ourselves. Don't those things matter, too?

If it feels like we have to perform a calculated dance just to get someone to pay attention to us, what do we actually have? You will never be able to convince someone to be interested in you. This is not an insult. It is an invitation to move forward and discover what's next. "He's just not that into you" doesn't matter nearly as much as whether or not *you* are into *him*. Are *you* actually interested in someone you're worried about "scaring away"? Is that really someone you want a substantial future with?

You get to lead. You get to drive. You don't have to spend your singlehood waiting around for someone to save you from it. You don't have to spend your singlehood performing elaborate calculations and dances to make people interested in you. Dating and relationships don't have to exhaust you to your wits' end. It gets to be easier than dating culture tells you it has to be.

The day I almost ran screaming from my laptop to go live in the forest forever was the first time I heard the term "catching feelings," as if feelings are a disease. Like it's a crime to actually like someone and become something more than a fucktoy for them. Yes, I just typed "fucktoy," and I didn't enjoy it any more than you did. Catching feelings?! How is that bad? Exactly how far gone is dating when *feeling things for people* is a negative? I'm sorry, but isn't developing feelings the *entire goddamned point?!* I'm so tired of the smoke and mirrors of modern dating. I think it's all exhausting, and I don't think we're getting a balanced return on our emotional and energetic investment.

Feel it. Feel it all. Like someone, and show it. It's okay. It's better than okay, because it's the truth. If anyone you're in contact with needs you to lie and minimize yourself in order to retain their attention, that person doesn't deserve one more second of it. I don't know if you've picked up on this, but life is kinda hard. I'm not in the mood to add a layer of dating game difficulty to it by having to pretend I don't give a shit about someone when really all I want is to go to the movies and then fool around on the couch. Whoever he is, I promise you if he needs you to lie to him by shrinking your feelings into as small and ignorable a package as possible, he is—quite frankly—a waste of your time.

You're not wrong for having feelings. You're not wrong for being yourself. You're not wrong for being single. When you can raise the value of what feels right to you, you can hold less space for everything else that feels wrong. You don't have to be anything other than your authentic self to be worthy of love. The right people for you won't be scared away by who you actually are, and you won't have to hide your real self forever to keep them around. That is the only version of a relationship that sounds as good or better than singlehood to me.

11

Shani's Singlehood Suggestions

We've talked a lot about reframing—the work we do inside ourselves to effect change in our thoughts and feelings. But that's not the only place loving and fully living single life happens.

Real-life singlehood scenarios often require an extra layer of effort, thought, and processing, because so much of the world is structured for couples. Singles, especially single women, often need foresight and extra energy to move smoothly through a world that would prefer we operate in sets of two. While I'm not afraid of a challenge, I am also a big fan of sharing what we've learned with our community.

Over the single years, I've picked up a few best practices that I think really help single women feel strong in their singlehood. They're not mandatory requirements, more like little morsels of wisdom you're free to sample as you please. I hope you find them helpful; I certainly have.

Part of singlehood is the notion that it's temporary. Singlehood is just a road that leads to Couple Town, right? (Give me strength.) I don't view us as temporary, but there are real-life consequences of the world seeing us that way. If we're viewed as temporary, less effort will be made to help us feel prepared, secure, and cared for every day. If it's assumed we're in a temporary state, why spend time and effort on something that's definitely going to change?

As someone who's been "temporary" for thirteen years now, I can assure you that tailoring your life to your single-hood is worth the effort. I don't deserve to live less comfortably and intentionally than anyone else, just because I'm a single woman. Whether you're single for another ten years or ten days, I want you to know this stuff, because it matters. You matter, just as you are now, not *only* once you've partnered. You are not temporary to me, whatever your relationship status is. While I'm on the topic, I don't want anyone to try and view singlehood as "permanent" either—just *valid*. Single life is valid, even if it's not how we'll live "forever."

"Forever" is such a bullshit word, by the way. Life is change, change is learning, and learning is wisdom. Whether you view change as good or bad, it's happening either way, so you might as well loosen your grip on the reins. Honestly, a stagnant life scares me far more than one full of change—but I know change is scary for many of us, and that's okay, too.

What follows are my favorite real-life pieces of advice for single women who will never learn them other than through experience, because the world doesn't really educate us on how to be single better. Why would it, when all it wants to do is shame us into searching harder for a husband so the dating industry as well as all other industries profiting off women's "flaws" can make more money? Anyway.

SAVINGS ACCOUNTS

Get and build a savings account. This is my number one piece of advice for single women. I suggest we build habits into our daily lives in service of growing savings and investment accounts. There are endless reasons why, but my favorite one is confidence. A savings account gives you the confidence to move through life knowing if shit hits the fan, you've got your own back. You don't have to depend on anyone else, and you don't have to ask anyone else for money, which can come with its own list of issues. More than anything, you're showing yourself a level of independence and capability that brings real benefits of freedom and safety along with it.

If you lose your job, you have an emergency fund. If an appliance breaks, you can replace it. If there's a family crisis somewhere, you can buy a plane ticket. If you want to self-publish a book perhaps, *you can*. A savings account is an insurance policy against all of life's little "what ifs," the ones that can generate a lot of fear and insecurity for single women. The knowledge your savings account is there—whatever its size—builds your confidence in your own ability to handle life. The fact that you're doing it on your own is one of the biggest boosts to your sense of solo okayness. It's a gift you give yourself.

So how do you build a savings account? Welp, you sure as shit talk to a financial advisor, not to me, but I'll tell you how I've been building mine—and I do acknowledge there are privileges in my life that allow me to do so. Every paycheck, without fail, I set aside a percentage I'm comfortable with. I started with a percentage that was *not* comfortable but grew to feel more secure over time. (Watching my money grow really helped with that.) I contribute one-third of every check I receive to a savings account. Every single time. (I'm independently employed, so this percentage accounts for what I'll need to pay in taxes as well.) This isn't about skipping a cup of coffee on your way to work. This is about designating a portion of your income to a savings account, as a matter of routine. You will never skip enough lattes to be able to afford a down payment. Attack your savings strategy at the source: your incoming money.

When my savings account hits a certain amount, I take out half of it and move it to an investment account with an investment app that's very easy for me to use, which allows my money to grow without any extra effort on my part. You don't need thousands of dollars to start an investment account, by the way. You can begin with a few hundred dollars. It's not about how much you start with; it's about starting *at all*. The money I've saved helps me grow *even more money*—and if you need a reason to get excited about developing savings habits, that's it. The investment app and my bank account are connected, so transfers and withdrawals are effortless.

A savings account is meant to be spent, which I know is counterintuitive, but remember all the work you've done to save has been for a reason. Use this money when you need it, because that's what it's there for. Allow the confidence you've built up over time as you've grown this account to reassure you that you'll put it all back in there eventually—and then some. Your savings can never grow unless you actually commit to contributing to it. This habit—not the dollars saved—is one of the most beneficial things I've done for myself while single.

Saving your money fortifies you against the mental and emotional stressors of life's "what if" moments. It also helps you handle them in a literal sense. *Fun fact*: couples have to save their money, too, because things can go awry even when you're in love.

PLANNING IN ADVANCE

The more we plan for, the less we worry about. Singlehood worries aren't something life prepares us for, so often singles can get caught off guard with a brand-new reason to panic. Fun, right? I love advanced planning for singles, because I love anything we do in service of our future selves feeling okay. What you plan for and how you plan will be up to you, but consider this a strong endorsement for thinking ahead.

I'm a lunatic, let's just start there, so I plan for everything—but especially weather. I am prepared for any form of disaster or inclement weather at literally all times. I stock emergency supplies in my home, and my go-bag could be featured on a reality television program about preppers. Don't let my personal fears of the forecast influence you too much, or do—it's your choice. The point is, whatever worries you the most, put things in place to plan for those outcomes. Have a fire or earthquake plan. Know the routes to local hospitals and how you'd get yourself there if you needed to go. Even if it's a "just in case" sort of thing, you'll feel better prepared than you'd feel unprepared.

There are other ways to prepare, and most of my favorites have to do with physical safety. I always carry backup cell phone batteries. When I own a car (which I haven't in eight years, but whatever), I have a AAA membership. I carry a variety of self-defense tools on my keychain; you can research them for yourself to find the right items for you. There have also been massive recent advancements in covert safety items like jewelry charms that alert emergency contacts and police/EMTs when activated. You can install cameras and security systems in your home with much more ease and affordability these days than a fully wired system.

Think about the things that concern you the most, and then put plans in place so that if they occur, you don't feel incapable, alone, or dependent on resources you can't access. Planning really does build your confidence while lowering your tendency to worry. This is smart stuff everyone should do, but I'm not worried about everyone right now—I'm invested in single women, and I want us to invest in ourselves and the security we feel when we're alone.

Another huge concern among singles is illness and eldercare planning. I have no expertise here, but many professionals do and can help you plan for unexpected or long-term illness, draft a power of attorney, set up a will, etc. I know this stuff is scary to talk about, but it's even scarier to think about when you simply don't know how things work or how they'd play out in an emergency. Shining a light on the scary bits by planning for them helps ease fear and tension. Remember: planning for these things doesn't mean they're definitely going to happen. It simply means you have peace of mind that if they do happen, you're prepared. You can always adjust these plans later, if and when you partner.

COMMUNITY

Right, friendship! Friends are awesome. Friends are, in my opinion, essential to living a happy and engaging single life. I love having friends of varying levels of closeness in my life. I love having friends all over the planet. I suggest prioritizing friendship in your life if you enjoy having people to do things with and talk to at parties. If you prefer being alone, that's cool, too!

Something you might not have thought about: our single friendships are the only friendships with a hole in the bucket—we have to keep filling it up. People partner; it happens. We actually *want* this to happen if partnership is what we want for ourselves, too, so try not to be sad when your single friends start seeing someone. You want that happiness for them because you want it for yourself as well. It makes sense.

If a friend starts spending a little less time with you once they start seeing someone, that's not an affront to you—it's just what's happening in their life. Adjust the friendship to fit the direction their life is taking, and know when the time comes, they will do the same for you. Or they won't, and maybe you don't need to be friends anymore. That's okay, too. We're allowed to make new friends, just as we're allowed to stay invested in the existing friendships we have, no matter where our lives take us. I'm a big fan of replenishing our single friendships as needed.

Community will not come to the single person. The single person must go to the community. When we need friendship, we have to put effort into finding it. Friendships and communities are not just going to materialize in front of us when we need them. We need to put effort into bringing the relationships that we want into our lives.

Hey, Shani, didn't you tell us that dating is one place where effort doesn't have to match reward? Why wouldn't that be true of making new friends?

Because it isn't. Friendship is different from dating, thank heavens. It's less charged. It's a different dynamic, and deciding to go to an oyster happy hour or book club

together is a lot easier than deciding to date monoga-
mously. Friendship is easier, and isn't that nice?

I'm asked, "How do I make new friends?" a hell of a lot
more often than, "How do I meet my partner?" and you
have no idea how much joy this brings me. As making new
friends is often easier than finding a partner, the methodol-
ogies for finding friendship have a higher success rate than
lookin' for love. I get that trying to make new friends can be
very intimidating and often filled with anxiety for many of
us. I'm never suggesting you put yourself in uncomfortable
situations. I'm simply saying if you want new friends, you'll
need to try and make them.

Hobbies and sports are an awesome route to friendship. Religious and spiritual organizations as well. Internet
friends are some of my favorites, and it is 100 percent possible to meet someone on a social media platform, never
hang out in real life, and still genuinely care about the
friendship. Obviously, real-life hanging out is better, but
when there's an ocean between you, do your best. Join
groups, attend events that interest you, and simply be
around other people to remind yourself that humans with
similar likes and curiosities actually exist!

An often untapped friendship resource: your existing
friends! It's entirely okay to reach out to friends you trust and
ask them if they have any friends or colleagues you should
meet. It's a vulnerable moment, for sure, but if someone
you care about hears you could use some new friendships
and doesn't respond positively, I'd be really surprised. I'd
also not want you to be friends with them anymore—ew.

We seem so comfortable asking our friends to set us up with potential lovers, so why not potential new friends? Let's also shed the limiting belief that if a friend introduces us to a new friend, we always have to include the introducer-friend in the plans. It's not cheating on the introducer-friend to hang out with the new friend alone. That was the whole point of being introduced to a new friend! But yeah, also include the introducer-friend sometimes, because that's a nice thing to do.

My point: if you want to make new friends, you have to try. Say hello. Introduce yourself. Ask someone where they got their cool shoes. Break the ice and put in the effort. Even if your efforts aren't rewarded with a new friend every single time, you got in some practice, and you should be proud of yourself.

HOBBIES

You have to do stuff. In addition to feeling a void in the friendship sector of our lives, I also hear from singles that sometimes...we're bored. Singlehood is a period of life that can often come with extra unscheduled blocks of time in our daily planners. Personally, I love unscheduled time— it makes me feel free and infinitely optimistic. But if it stresses you out or makes you feel a bit untethered, you need some hobbies.

Hobbies are something you look forward to doing. They're not just time-fillers you put up with because it's "something to do." Take your time, do a little research, and ask around. You'll know you found the right hobby when you look forward to it, when you don't notice time passing while you're doing it, and those feelings of emptiness or boredom when you have free time dissipate. Free time should be something we look forward to—rather than something we fear because we're single and feel a big, intimidating gap in our lives. Having "nothing going on" in our lives is a choice, and we can choose to make a different one by finding new things to do.

The actual hobbies you take up will be uniquely your choice. Some people like to garden, others hate dirt and bugs. Maybe you're athletic and want to try some new sports or classes. I'm about as athletic as a fiddle-leaf fig, so my hobbies are often of the crafty or creative nature. I love to read—that counts as a hobby! I also hope buying books and then letting them pile up on my coffee table because I can't possibly read them all that fast counts as a hobby, too, because I'm *great at it.*

This is a really long-winded way of saying "find stuff to do," but...find stuff to do. It helps make single life feel fuller where once you may have felt differently.

PETS

Unless you're allergic to all living creatures, get a pet. I cannot stress this enough. Pets (and plants if your landlord says you can't have pets!) are a single person's first line of defense against feeling alone. Singles love adopting a pet! We're pet people! A pet is someone in the house all the time, who loves you and snuggles you and doesn't complain when you dress them up in themed outfits like a human might. We're a population of human beings who aren't bothered by the need to lint roll ourselves on our way out the door—bring on the pets!

Seriously speaking, the companionship of a pet is priceless. My cat, Clementine (longtime fans of my work will wonder how I made it this far in the book without mentioning her), was with me for twelve years, through the darkest days of my singlehood, and she was my family. She was the reason I was never sad to come home after work or from a trip. Even if she didn't always admit it, she was happy to see me every time I walked in the door, or even in the room—which felt really nice. She was the reason I felt sturdy during scary times, too. If there was a blizzard or, you know, a pandemic, Clem was there both to keep me company and to give me purpose. Needing to take care of her and make sure she was safe was something that brought me a sense of importance, and I think that's okay.

There's a comfort and companionship you can only find in pets. Adopting mine was one of the best decisions I've ever made, and to the extent you're able, I highly recommend adopting a furball of some kind. Or a lizard, whatever.

CUSTOMIZATION

Please remember how little compromise is involved in being single. It is perhaps our greatest magical power. Think about all the things you've done and all the decisions you've made in the last week alone. Then think about never having to factor in another human being when making those decisions. Everything from dinner plans, to Netflix options, to the order in which you run errands, even the temperature in your home—you made these decisions completely independently of the opinions of another person.

You didn't need anyone to agree with you. You didn't have to *convince* anyone to agree with you. The time we save in never having to compromise is itself a gift of singlehood. There is no burden of adjusting what we *really* want in order to hold space for someone else. Compromise is awesome, and I'm not saying there's anything wrong with it—it's just that you don't have to do it while you're single, and I think we should enjoy the situation at hand. It's all up to you, all the time, which allows singles to live some truly customized lives.

My fear is we'll spend this single time so heads-down in dating apps, so dedicated to the hunt for a partner, that we'll miss out on how tailored to our own tastes and wants our single lives can be. There's a *lot* of freedom and fun here, and I don't want us to ignore it. Being in a (good) relationship is wonderful, for sure. Until that happens, though, you might just want to do whatever the fuck you want.

Example: Halloween is entirely my shit. My dream house would look sort of like the Addams Family's next real estate investment. One year, when I was putting away the Halloween decorations, I was sad. I didn't want to have to wait a year for some of my favorite pieces of haunted decor to come out again. So I didn't. I left them where they stood, and now there are several pieces of Halloween decor that are simply a part of my permanent style around the house. Maybe you can pack a glittering black candelabra away in a box for eleven months, but I can't.

Top to bottom, all the decisions about where and how you live are yours. Again, these aren't temporary lives we're living; these are our present-day, real lives that can be entirely designed to bring us joy.

Here's a good exercise, if you're having trouble envisioning a more customized life: walk into your kitchen and ask yourself how many things are where they are because that's where Mom or Dad says they go. Is there a placement for the salt and pepper shakers that's more convenient for you personally? Apart from leaving things where they are for sentimental reasons, it can be quite freeing to decide for yourself that the Windex should actually live under the bathroom sink instead. It might seem like a small thing, but these little acts of personalization are reframing steps themselves. They're claiming and customizing your space and your time, and they feel really, really good. The more single life goodness we can show ourselves, the easier it is to stop trying to run from singlehood, because we get to appreciate it instead.

A quick word on not wanting to let your whole self shine in the way you live and operate, lest it "scare away" potential partners. I have considered the fact that a fake raven skeleton in a spooky cloche from Target sitting on my bookshelf might freak out a date or two. Remember: if someone *can* be scared away by your authentic self, they should go ahead and leave. The right future partner for me will not only approve of my Halloween style, he'll likely also look forward to helping me increase my collection.

ASSEMBLY AND REPAIRS

You are 100 percent free to ignore everything in this section and revert back to the Savings Account Philosophy when things break or need installing by simply hiring someone to do the work for you. That's allowed and still counts as being resourceful. If, however, you take great joy in being entirely self-sufficient to the tune of learning how to cut your own bangs like your ol' pal Shani, it's time to get comfortable with assembly and repairs. I have assembled more pieces of furniture by myself than I can recall in any detail. Is putting furniture together alone a massive pain in the ass? Yep! Does that mean you should avoid it and settle for a folding table in your dining room? No chance in hell.

Watch a tutorial, take class, ask a friend, use trial and error—I don't care, learn how to solve small problems around the house that are within the average untrained person's capability. If your kitchen sink starts spewing purple goo instead of water, definitely call a plumber—but if you need to hang artwork or shelves, install a security camera, or replace the legs on your favorite vintage chair, you've got this. I strongly suggest every single woman invest in a toolkit and get comfortable using it. (Might I also suggest a power drill? Use one. You'll understand my admiration.) Assembling furniture alone will always be a massive annoyance, but annoying and impossible are two very different things. One of my proudest moments working in the singlehood space was when one of my podcast listeners assembled an entire patio furniture set—I'm talking a full outdoor living room—by herself after purchasing a set she thought came fully assembled. If she's reading this right now, well done, madam.

The feeling of accomplishment you get from doing something necessary and maybe previously a little intimidating contributes to your overall comfort and happiness as a single woman. You did that, by yourself—it's a big deal! Accomplishments of this kind feel good and reiterate to us that even if we wish we weren't alone, it's okay that we are—we can handle things. We're not trying to get to a place where we don't "need anyone," because that's just unnecessary. Need people all you want. We're humans, and community is kind of our thing. But when your kitchen table wobbles or you're getting a weird draft from a window, you don't have to feel helpless as though the only solution is to just accept it and be uncomfortable because "there's no one around to fix it." You are around. You can fix things. And it feels affirming and wonderful when you do.

COPING SKILLS

Every now and then, things go apeshit. All the advanced planning in the world can't stop the unknowns and unstoppables of life from happening. That doesn't mean we are totally helpless and entirely fucked when they go down. Coping skills are things you develop that are specific to you that you call in off the bench when you're having a tough time.

Dating is hard, and being single can be hard—and that's on totally normal days. As singles, we also have to deal with the extreme days alone, too, but I want to very clearly communicate to you that we *can* deal with them. It is possible.

Coping skills can be anything from contacting a therapist to meditating to hitting a punching bag for a while. Some enjoy long walks, self-massage, or creating art. Baking is one of my coping skills, as it requires my mind to focus on something creative and productive, and I feel like I'm giving my nervous system a little break from freaking out, which eases things for me. I also love music. Sometimes gentle sound is really soothing during times of anxiety and stress. I pretty much always have incense burning in my home, because scent is a big thing for me and my mood (and I've learned that incense gives you much more bang for your buck than candles—fun fact).

What I want to emphasize here is there are ways to cope with tough times that don't necessarily require having a partner to lean on. They don't even require having friends or family to lean on! Obviously, call your support system when you need to, but I want you to know that we have within us the *capability* to handle things on our own, too. Alone is not helpless, stranded, or without options. Too often, we fear "alone," but I think it's something we can be proud of. Think of all you've done alone already, and use your own personal history as proof that you can handle difficult times should they arise.

There are many ways to come by an education. I spent thirteen years getting my doctorate in single life. My areas of specialty will probably be different from yours, and I have no doubt you've learned a *ton* through single living, too! Share your wisdom with your single community, and help each other move through life with a bit more ease, comfort, and confidence.

Singlehood isn't a lesser life. It isn't resigning to a life that's harder or lonelier than the lives of others. We are not temporary and therefore unworthy of adjusting our lives to our own comfort. Understanding and leaning into the value of our singlehood by learning and adjusting in order to feel confident is a massive step toward living with more happiness and ease every *single* day.

Window-Shoppers

We need to talk about hurting people's feelings. While I don't advocate for walking around being a flagrant asshole to people for no reason, I do think that we need to give less of a shit about the feelings of others. This sounds weird, I know. But how many times have you avoided *possibly* hurting someone's feelings even though your feelings were *definitely* already infringed upon in the first place? I think we've been groomed as women to put our feelings and needs behind those of others. I think sometimes, we're human sponges, absorbing pain and discomfort and awkwardness caused by other people so that they themselves don't have to experience the fallout of their own actions. Sounds insane when you see it typed out, doesn't it?

This behavior looks like putting other people first, when it costs you something—when you are uncomfortable, put out, or emotionally hurt in some way, but you don't do anything about it, because you don't want the other person, who *caused* that discomfort, to feel bad or embarrassed. When's the last time you just laughed off an unwanted advance in public because you didn't want to "make a scene" or insult the feelings of the person inappropriately coming on to you? How many times have you said nothing because you didn't want someone to "feel bad" about what they'd said or done?

It's not always that direct, or even that intense. There are passive ways we put other people before ourselves, too. I think these passive infringements upon our feelings can add up to be a bigger deal, actually. One of my favorite examples of single women putting their feelings in a dusty box under the bed while polishing someone else's feelings on the mantle is what I call "window-shopping."

"Window-shopping" is a term I use for those dudes you almost dated but didn't really, but kind of talked to for a while or maybe got drinks with late one night because he was already out with friends so it was a "group thing" and he didn't feel threatened or cornered by the idea of an actual date, because he doesn't actually want to date just one woman—why on earth would he when online dating is his own personal buffet of sex and attention?

Anyway.

A person window-shops you when they follow you on Instagram and view all your Instagram stories but never actually have any direct contact with you of any kind. You might get a like on a photo. *Maybe*. This can occur on other social media platforms in various ways, but really all that's happening is this person has full access to every part of your life that you choose to share, without ever having to exert any effort to be a real part of that life. These people are bottom-feeding on the very easiest, least-effort-required way to consume you—because they have an *interest* in consuming you, as long as it doesn't require them to, you know, do anything.

Why do we allow this?

And yes, I mean *allow*. I've used the word "allow" several times now, and I want us to pay attention to how it makes us feel. It's a little uncomfortable! So much outlandish bullshit that we don't deserve happens to single women in the dating space that it's uncomfortable for us to think we somehow had a hand in it. The single and dating space has a dynamic within it where things, often not-so-good things, happen *to* us. He didn't text back. She ghosted. They showed up to the date in a stained T-shirt and flip-flops even though you dressed nicely for the occasion (really happened to me once). Of course, we don't move through the world inviting foul manners like unwanted dick pics and rude texts. But when these things happen, where are *we*? The other people in these scenarios made their choices, so now what? Will we allow things we're not okay with to continue, or will we make different choices?

As I'm sure you've noticed, reframing our singlehood in order to feel good about it, and stop feeling like we have to cure it as fast as possible by any means necessary, has a lot to do with agency and choice. It also involves remembering we don't have to be in a passive position simply because we're single. When things happen that we don't like, we can decide what happens next.

We (and I include iterations of myself here, so don't think I'm judging you—I *am* you) allow window-shopping for a very simple reason: attention feels good. We are human, and human beings like attention, praise, adoration, and love, and yes, we enjoy Instagram likes. It's why the entire app exists: we become addicted to approval—it's fine. You can fight it if you want to, but unless you have a better alternative, social media is winning. How you choose to behave on social media is how *you* win.

We allow people, specifically people we at one point probably wanted to be involved with romantically, to window-shop us because it's attention, and it is a form of praise. These next sentences are going to sound like I'm shaming you—I'm not. I'm listing them here so that you know the mood I'm referencing. There is no shame, just truth, especially since by the end of this chapter, you're going to block these asshats and move on with your life.

Have you ever:

- been happy "he" looked at your story?
- seen significance in the fact that he looked at your story with no other evidence of significance than the viewing of the story itself?
- posted something hoping he would see it?

- thought if you posted the "right" thing, he'd get in touch?
- thought if you posted the "right" thing, you'd be together?
- felt disappointed when he didn't get in touch?
- felt frustrated because none of them ever get in touch?
- thought having your Instagram stories viewed by window-shoppers was better than nothing?

If any of this sounds familiar, welcome! You're a human person—happy to have you. All of these thoughts are completely valid and human, but because these thoughts also lead to or already indicate low self-worth, we don't have to keep having them. We can retrain our brains and emotions around them, because the window-shoppers' feelings don't come first; yours do.

Window-shopping is not better than nothing. It is worse than nothing, because it's nowhere near what you actually want. And when we allow window-shopping, we show ourselves it's okay to settle for something that's *so much less* than what we want. If you want a relationship but settle for Instagram story views, something needs to change—and thankfully, that change is really easy to implement.

Block them! That's the change. You have a block button at your disposal, and you should block every last one of your window-shoppers, right fucking now. You have the choice to revoke any access to you that they are not earning.

Maybe this is a bit of an unseen benefit, but blocking window-shoppers doesn't just block their access to you. It also removes them from your headspace as well, because they haven't actually earned *that* either. That's the real emotional papercut for me when it comes to window-shoppers: when they occupy real estate in our brains, rent-free, and instead cost us the disappointment of remembering this person we wanted something to happen with, but nothing ever did. Remember: every time you see they viewed your story, you're thinking about them. You're allowing them to pop back into your head, even if only for a moment.

You can free your social media space and your own damned thoughts from someone who isn't earning the right to be in either place. Window-shoppers are taking your time, energy, and effort, and they're giving you 0.5 seconds of their viewing time in return while they're taking a shit. Your self-worth can do a whole lot better than that.

Again, no shame, but have you ever:

- felt guilty for blocking someone because of how they might feel when they find out they're blocked?
- not wanted to block someone because that means the end of that attention?
- figured it would just be easier to allow them to continue to follow you?
- worried about not being able to window-shop *them*, too?

It's totally okay to think these things, but now it's time to ask yourself what these thoughts are really saying to you.

- Why are you prioritizing another person's possibly disappointed feelings regarding being blocked over your own actually disappointed feelings because they never try to be in your life in a real way? Why are their feelings more important than yours?

- Why are you settling for the smallest morsel of attention possible? Do you want more? Then stop accepting less. You can't get more from window-shoppers. Here's proof: have you ever?

- Why are you afraid to take a very simple action that can give you back tenfold in self-worth benefits by removing people who only maybe sort of want to see stuff you post? It's actually much harder to continue feeling like shit than it is to no longer have someone popping up in your head in a disappointing, wanting, lacking way all the time.

- Why do you give time and headspace to someone who shows you, over and over again, that the only effort you're worth to them is something as effortless as an Instagram story view?

Is window-shopping enough for you? It isn't enough for me. The most minor moments of attention aren't enough for me, not when what I really want is my next relationship. Window-shoppers are giving us crumbs, and when we keep letting them window-shop, we're settling for them.

You were not put on this earth to settle for social media views from guys who don't remember your real name unless it's in your Instagram handle. You're here to have everything you want. Stop settling for crumbs. Block. Block them all.

How often are we motivated by not wanting other people to "feel bad"? Feeling bad is just guilt in cuter shoes. Society gives us enough guilt about being single in the first place, so I really want us as single women to avoid the further guilt that comes from centering the feelings of other people while doing nothing about our own feelings at the same time.

Self-worth is what supports you in taking actions that can feel scary. When you know you are worth more than an Instagram story view, you don't feel bad about blocking someone, nor do you feel bad about how long you let them have access to you in the first place. Your self-worth knows that this is all an education, that we're always growing and developing. We don't learn how to do anything unless we try and practice. Every time you block someone, you're practicing. You're showing yourself you can block people who haven't earned their access to you, and the world won't end. You make room in your head for more than someone giving you the bare minimum of attention.

Each action you take in service of your self-worth helps it grow. And it will grow! Self-worth-driven actions feel great, because each time, you prove to yourself that you can put your feelings first. Reaping the benefits helps you take more and more of these actions in the future, with less and less guilt.

Self-worth is not arrogance—I want to make that clear, since mischaracterizing self-worth is another sneaky way the world trains women to put other people first. Self-worth isn't a superiority complex. It's knowing your own validity, that you matter just as much as everyone else, that no one matters more than you, and that your singlehood doesn't somehow place you at a lesser value than other human beings. It is not arrogant to know your worth and to require other people to respect you. I know we worry about coming across as arrogant or superior just for wanting the world to treat us with respect. But anyone who sees my self-worth as arrogance is someone who was benefiting from me having no self-worth at all.

I want you to really think about something, and don't be ashamed, because you're reading this by yourself and no one can see you: do you really want a relationship that started because you happened to post the "right" thing on Instagram, the one photo that made someone "snap out" of the passive, zero-effort opinion they had of you and into a magical realm of "Omg, I want her immediately?" Don't be ashamed for ever having thought this; just find out what it feels like to be proud of yourself for blocking your god-damned window-shoppers.

Self-worth doesn't care when you show up; it's just so happy to have you at the party. When you block window-shoppers, you give yourself little examples of how good it can feel to have agency over your own presence in the world and in the dating space. Remember: you are in charge of who has access to you on social media. Make sure everyone who has that access deserves it.

Social media is good at getting us to settle for scraps. So is the modern dating world. When those two forces team up, they eat our self-worth on toast. Do not be the one who serves it to them. Take back your agency over who has access to you. Define what it takes to be a part of your life, and know that anyone who can't rise to those requirements isn't meant to be with you anyway.

Imagine if all of us blocked window-shoppers and told bad actors in the dating space that they aren't allowed to treat us with disrespect. What would it look like to participate in the dating world if there were more manners and balance? Players in the dating space engage in shitty behaviors because they can. I don't want them to get away with it, but I can only be in one place at a time, so I'm going to need your help on this. I know you're worth more, and I want you to know it, too. Let's all expect more from the digital and real worlds around us than we've been led to believe we can expect. Let me see our self-worth shining, rather than settling for scraps. I want to see it.

Delete Your Dating Apps

Here we are. I'm finally going to say it. There's no gentle way to go about this, and quite frankly, if you're currently using dating apps, you're not exactly being treated gently, so why tiptoe? This chapter will speak directly to singles who are not enjoying dating apps. This is for those who would equate their dating app experience with what it might feel like to be bitten repeatedly by piranhas while swimming in a pond full of trash and pointy sticks. You're not having a good time is what I'm saying.

If you're someone who *enjoys* the apps and finds success on them—whatever you deem success to be—then feel free to skip straight over this chapter, because it's not for you. Also, congratulations on being a mystical unicorn. When I say delete your dating apps, I say it to those of us in dating app hell, who still—for some reason—can't let the damn things go.

I'm not going to be delicate or wishy-washy (a term I can't say out loud without laughing) about my thoughts on dating apps. My thoughts on dating apps come from ten years of experience with them, plus several more years working in a community of women still experiencing them. The behaviors and encounters single women are exposed to (joke extremely intended) in the dating app world are abhorrent, and while love and marriage are incredible things, I don't think surviving the hell of app life is a prerequisite for finding them. If you've ever wandered into a dating app quagmire and found yourself asking, "Why does it have to be this hard?!" I am here to tell you it actually doesn't. I hope this is welcome news to you, though the solution might be a bit harder to handle.

I think single women should delete their dating apps. All of them, forever. I'm not going to talk about statistics or data surrounding online dating. Not because that stuff isn't interesting or factual, but because there's a much simpler and more logical way to make my point. Dating apps are a business. They exist to make money. They are not driven by an altruistic desire to help you "find love," because the moment you do, they lose a customer.

Why would someone you give money to want you to stop giving them money? How are dating apps incentivized to actually help you find a partner? They're not. They're incentivized to help you do the exact opposite. Dating apps themselves don't want this to dawn on us, but I bet cigarette companies weren't wild about the first anti-smoking campaigns, either.

The first thing you have to reframe, if you're going to consider permanently releasing yourself from the shitbog of dating apps, is: *How will I meet someone?* That's the big question single women are too scared to address, because anything that could potentially lead to love is an option we've been groomed to believe is viable. If someone told a miserably single woman she'd meet someone hanging out at a shoe repair shop, she'd pay the owner rent to stand in the corner. And how could we blame her? The longer you date and date and date and date to no avail, the more willing you become to try *anything*. It is my sincere hope that you will also try what I'm suggesting, because this actually works—once you change what it is you're trying so hard to fix.

I'm not trying to fix your singlehood with a relationship. I'm trying to fix your unhappiness about your singlehood by helping you let go of an industry that's taking advantage of it.

We've been taught by modern dating culture that dating apps are "the way everyone meets now." They've been held out to us as a mandatory activity that single people must participate in, because to abstain would be akin to a life of solitude.

"But...if we don't use the apps, how will we meet someone?! We'll never meet someone if we don't use the apps!"

A simple reframe: Are you meeting "someones" now? Are you really starting relationships as a result of online dating? I'm guessing no, because you're reading this book, so honestly, what do you have to lose, apart from the endless uncomfortable, unfair, exhausting situations you've been living through—potentially for years—that result in all your little horror stories?

Are dating apps serving you? Have they ever? Then why do you keep allowing them to be a part of your life? As I've mentioned, I deleted my accounts and my apps in early 2019, and I have never felt compelled to get them back. I want you to know that this is possible. I've completely eliminated the pull to redownload that we're all so familiar with by acknowledging that the apps never, ever, *ever* gave me anything but disappointment at best, and horror stories at worst.

I stopped believing in a dating app fantasy and started listening to what they were actually telling me instead.

The modern dating app experience is a mechanical, degrading, exhausting endeavor where "success" is someone else's fairy tale and horror stories are now the norm. And yes, people do meet via dating apps. Of course they do. But have you? Or have you just been slogging through bullshit for years on end, convinced something will eventually work out? He isn't one swipe away because he never has been, despite the thousands of chances you've given dating apps with your money and your thumbs. But dating apps are really good at making us believe all it's going to take is just one more swipe, and then another paid boost, and then another upgrade to where the people you might actually want are hidden, and then more swiping. We're the rabbit, a partner is the carrot, and dating apps dangle it on a string in front of our faces to see how long we'll chase it. I'm sorry, pay to chase it.

I don't say this to make us feel like idiots. I'm fully aware of how harsh these words can sound—I said them to myself long before I said them to you. Everything is said with love, respect, and a genuine desire for our lives to get better. I say all this to help us forgive ourselves. That feeling of addiction, like you *have to* redownload the apps, is by design. Dating apps are designed to make you think you need them, but they're never obligated to give you the thing you actually want. You don't need them. We don't need them. We'll talk about why.

I don't see the point in addressing this problem by speaking to the people making money off of it—because they're never incentivized to change. I'd much rather speak to the people *giving them the money*, and potentially make a goddamned difference.

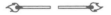

If most of the screenshots I see posted in online groups for single women were seen by the senders' bosses, an overwhelming number of single men in this country would be out of work. The cozy blanket of dating app anonymity insulates the public from seeing the repeated verbal, emotional, mental, and sexual abuse of women. Imagine if before he could send you a message, or include something in his profile, he had to tweet it first.

Dating app behavior has only gotten bolder over time, because it can. Bad manners build on consequenceless bad manners, and they intensify. Unfortunately, people who get away with bad behavior aren't ever likely to change it, unless incentivized. Your boss who's massively underpaying you isn't just going to spontaneously give you a raise out of "the goodness of their heart." No, you're going to keep being underpaid until you demand more or quit.

Your dating app membership should come with real mental and emotional support, but so far, the only tangible aid or defense single women have is a block button. What the block button doesn't account for is you have to experience the bad thing *before* you can block someone. It has to happen to you—you have to live through it first—before you can block the individual who knew he could do what he did with little to no consequence. Dating app culture is one where men (that's who's doing it most of the time—I feel comfortable saying "men") feel at ease putting in minimal effort and maximum offense. They feel comfortable doing whatever they please, because they know why women are using dating apps. When women are looking for partnership, men who are looking for sex are more than willing to take advantage of the situation. It's an ecosystem of competing goals and a *private place* to treat women however the fuck they want. I made the choice to stop participating in this complete bullshit, and every part of my life improved as a result.

You're giving dating apps your attention, time, and most often, your money. What are you getting in return? Is it anything? Is it anything positive? When we accept singlehood as a lesser life status, we become willing to put up with anything, for any amount of time, if we think there's a chance it will lead to partnership. How long are you willing to give dating apps a chance, while they see the reprehensible manners and behavior you experience as a totally normal part of using their product? They've had years to *actually* fix this shit. They've never bothered.

After a decade of use—and believe me, I wish I'd asked myself these questions earlier—I was finally able to see dating apps weren't serving me in any capacity. In ten years, all they'd given me was emotional and mental pain and exhaustion. I was finally able to see them as a pointless presence in my life, which made it so much easier than it had ever been to remove them. I no longer considered them a path to partnership, because they'd never once delivered on that offering. They had only ever been a path to misery, and why would I voluntarily bring suffering into my life?

Please understand that dating apps are for-profit businesses. The last thing a business wants you to do is to stop using its product. Just the opposite—it wants you to use it a lot, for a long time, and if it's really smart, it will get you to think you need it. A hair dye company will never try to convince you that gray hair is beautiful. (It is, by the way.) They'd lose money if they did that. Instead, they'll support the societally accepted idea that gray hair is "old" or "ugly," and sell you a product that "fixes" it. In doing so, they lock in repeat customers for *decades*. A lot of industries make a lot of money helping women fix things that aren't wrong. Many of them, like the dating and diet industries (please read *The F*ck It Diet* by Caroline Dooner, by the way) are actually incentivized *never* to solve the problem they want you to think you have.

The couples who actually meet and form partnerships via dating apps are always used as bait to get struggling singles back in the mosh pit, because there is no better bait on Earth than romantic love. In addition to it just feeling amazing, our society has made romantic love and sex between two monogamous partners the most celebration-worthy thing there is. The only party bigger than a wedding is the fucking Oscars. Of course, apps use the couples who meet on their platforms to hold on to the business of everyone who doesn't. There's nothing the marketing team at a dating app loves more than a happy, attractive couple they can trot out like prized livestock. And if they can't find one attractive enough, believe me—they'll fake it.

It's the cruelest taunt. *"Well, I found my husband on a dating app, and I don't have to use dating apps anymore, so you'd better go use dating apps more!"* Hearing why I should do something painful and optional from someone who no longer has to do something painful and optional is really goddamned annoying, if I'm honest.

I'm so tired of a "success story" every now and then translating to literally millions of people swiping their lives away. Happy couples who are currently together because they met via online dating are little more than an algorithmic accident. For heaven's sake, even a broken clock is right twice a day. *Obviously, some people* are going to meet in a space where millions and millions of people hang out. Congratulations, dating apps—you built the world's biggest imaginary bar scene.

Happy couples are the best-case scenario for human beings, and the worst-case scenario for dating apps themselves. When two people on a dating app fall in love, the app stops making money off of them. *Why would it want that?*

When you move from a place of shame and lack around your own singlehood to a place where you can see its value, dating apps can't prey on your hope and make billions from it anymore.

> Old thought: *If I delete my dating apps, I'll be single longer.*
> New thought: *If I delete my dating apps, I'll be happier for however long my singlehood lasts.*

Why do we think dating apps are a faster solution to singlehood even when we've already spent *years* using them to no avail? Deleting your dating apps is not the same as "choosing singlehood." Deleting your dating apps is choosing to take something that's making you unhappy and stop giving it access to your life.

Online dating isn't made for the people who meet their partners. It's made for those of us who never do. It will take our money, time, and self-worth forever, if we let it. I spent ten years, god knows how much money, and every ounce of my self-worth on dating apps. For a long time, I didn't know which one I valued most, but now I know that my self-worth is the most priceless item. If I lose it, I put myself in very real danger of signing up for a lifetime of settling. Dating apps literally convinced me to lower my standards to meet *their* fabricated reality.

There is an idea that endless scrolling and swiping plants in our minds like a deleted scene from *Inception*. One simple idea, that time spent single + age = less worth. Because you've been swiping forever and still haven't found someone (because the apps don't want you to), you might internalize that "failure" as a need to lower your standards.

When you believe that lie, when you let the people partnering up around you combine with the societal shame of still being single, and when you let "Why are you still single?" take root in your brain, your brain will team up with the apps. It will start to tell you that you're asking for too much, because you're not enough to want what you want. If you were, wouldn't you have found it by now? Remember: *the dating apps don't want you to find someone.* They make more money if you don't.

If we internalize our dating app experience and think it's our fault for being undesirable or unlovable, instead of the apps' fault for being fundamentally shit, we lower our standards, over and over again, thinking if we don't, we'll be single longer. We start to think we have to take what we can get, because we haven't gotten anything yet. Instead of entertaining the idea that maybe online dating isn't designed to work for us, but instead for itself, we start to believe we're doing something wrong. I'm pretty sure making victims think everything is their own fault is something abusers do.

When I was online dating, I found myself in an endless spiral of "standards lowering." I would take away one desire after another, telling myself that because I hadn't "found him yet," I didn't have any choice but to lower my expectations. Rock bottom looked something like "I'll take anyone," a thought that turns my stomach now that I've come to understand the value of singlehood itself. Now that I understand being single isn't inherently a bad thing, I can recognize I wasn't online dating for a decade—I was avoiding disaster in the form of settling that entire time.

When I was spiraling and thought the only way out of the problem of singlehood was lowering my standards to fit whatever was still willing to go out with me, I'd go on dates with "anyone," only to be completely disappointed in them and myself. Because the thing about lowering your standards and settling is when you decide to settle on your life partner, you have to settle forever. This isn't Pepsi being okay; this is the rest of your life spent lying to yourself, convincing yourself to want someone, or worse still, believing something you don't want is the best you can have. To me, that mindset felt like a prison of disappointment, and by online dating, I was voluntarily walking inside.

Now, more than two years app-free, I can see how I was letting a system designed to keep me single make me think I had to lower my standards, so I was only ever connecting with people I had no interest in, and so on into infinity—or at least until I woke the fuck up. I was the ideal dating app user. I was buying the bullshit and playing right into the industry's ones and zeroes. I kept bringing myself and my standards lower, and lower, and lower, and dating apps kept meeting me exactly where I was: the bottom. They were thrilled to have me (and my money) right there.

The last thing a dating app wants you to understand is singlehood is wonderful. It's a priceless time in your life—for however long it lasts. It is free, full, and endlessly variable. It belongs to you and no one else. It is compromise-free and curiosity-packed. It is completely tailored to how you want to live it, without needing anyone else on board with how *you* want to live.

Understanding this makes swiping your adulthood away seem like a comical waste of time. If and when you make the decision to delete your dating apps, remember to forgive yourself for any time, money, and emotional energy you spent on them. It wasn't for nothing—nothing is ever for nothing. Everything, every day, is an education. Dating apps count as education, too, and because they don't hand out spouses like diplomas, you can decide when it's time to matriculate the fuck out.

I don't hate my singlehood, much to societal shame and dating apps' disappointment. I have learned to see its value, to cherish its preciousness, and to deeply feel its freedom and joy. I know I won't be single forever, so I want to cherish this time while I've got it. Did you know valuing the single time in your life was even an option? Or had shame and lack forced you to see it as only something to fix as fast as possible, and at any cost?

Whoever they are, the person I partner with will have to be amazing to get me to give up my singlehood—and they should be, if I'm going to spend a significant portion of my life with them. Dating apps wanted me to hate being single, and they gave themselves a repeat customer by being a massive reason why I hated being single in the first place.

Being single, at any age and for any length of time, isn't an indicator that we need to lower our expectations. It's an invitation to fully love single life and refuse to give it up for anything less than something just as awesome or better. We don't feel compelled to spend our time digging through dating apps when we love single life—which is actually quite easy to love, when we stop swiping long enough to allow ourselves to.

1 4

The S Word

I don't believe in single women settling. At this point, I think I've made that at least a little bit clear. I don't believe we're lesser beings, and I don't believe our singleness indicates we're doing life wrong. I just don't see the flaws and faults society assigns to us. So I don't believe in settling, because I don't think we have to.

What is settling, really? What does settling look and feel like? While it will be different for everyone, there are certainly commonalities. The most common theme running through settling is something we settle for being a lesser version of what we actually wanted. Or, settling is accepting a version of what we wanted that's...wait for it..."good enough." The phrase "good enough," when used in reference to single women makes my heart crumple like notebook paper.

It's the idea that we're wrong for wanting, and for maintaining expectations at the same levels that everyone who partnered before us set theirs. I find the idea of settling, or the suggestion we should settle, extremely insulting. My singleness doesn't make me less worthy than anyone else. I don't care if I've been single for thirteen years or thirty. My value is not determined by whether or not there are two names on my electric bill. My singleness is my freedom, my independence, and my gift—it is not my flaw. I will not give it up for anyone who isn't *at least* as wonderful as my singlehood is. I sure as shit won't settle for someone who's less so.

So much single shaming comes from the ways single women are perceived, which can have a massive impact on how we see ourselves. These perceptions can trick us into thinking we *have to* settle, because we're single, which is wrong and bad—so what business do we have expecting anything better? I know this feeling, far too well, and I want to make it clear that we aren't giving it to ourselves—we're absorbing it from outside of us, and it's well within our capability to let it fucking go.

Honestly, if society can't get it together and start seeing single women as valid, worthy, and *lucky*, we're going to have to get the ball rolling for them. One thing we do *not* have to do on society's behalf is settle—in any area of life. We have the ability to decide how we view ourselves and our singlehood, independent of society's single shaming.

Society is a group of people and a set of views that aren't actually living our lives. How does our settling or not settling actually affect them? And why do their opinions of us have to impact our own? Why can't our opinions of ourselves impact *them*?

Settling is wanting one thing but telling yourself that less, sometimes much less, is enough. Settling is telling ourselves that we can't expect something as good as what we want, because we're not as good as other people who are already in couples. Settling for less because we view singlehood as a lower life status, because we view ourselves as "taking too long" to "find someone," is bullshit—understandable, relatable bullshit, but bullshit nonetheless.

I don't want shame to motivate my decisions, and I don't want it to motivate yours, either. I want you to know it doesn't have to.

Not settling isn't the same as choosing to be single forever. Nothing you do ever implies you're choosing permanent singlehood (unless you're actually choosing to be single forever, which is of course a choice that's available to you if you want it). Societal messages of urgency and failure—you know, the ones that make us feel like rapidly expiring dairy products—can drive us to settle. Our society holds singlehood in *such low regard* that a lifetime of settling sounds better than a lifetime of singlehood. To this I say...barf.

I swear on a stack of Judy Blume novels that I would rather wake up every day for the rest of my life next to a pile of cats I genuinely love as opposed to a man I'm forcing myself to.

Singlehood is not a commandment to settle. In my opinion, it's just the opposite. It's the freedom and time to discover what we want, and never settle for less. When we appreciate and value singlehood, we won't leave it for anything less than what we actually want—and we won't feel like we have to.

Why would we ever settle if we saw the value in single life? When you see single life for all that it actually is, you don't settle for one-word text messages, or men who string you along with promises of spending time with you "next week." You don't settle for someone with whom you see multiple red flags. You don't settle for someone you don't feel any actual desire for but spend time with anyway simply because he's... there. Not settling is a really awesome side effect of shedding limiting, false, shame-driven beliefs about singlehood.

You don't deserve a future you settled for. You don't deserve to wake up every morning disappointed by how your life turned out. You don't deserve to spend your adulthood wondering how different things could have been but won't be because you settled just so you didn't have to be single anymore. Settling is not better than singlehood. The world won't tell you that, but I will.

Now that we know what settling is, why do we do it? In my experience, single women settle because we fear the future.

Fear of the future is looking ahead in your life, imagining how things could be for you, and feeling afraid. Fear of the future leads single people to accept less than we want, because we're scared nothing else is coming. We stop hoping or trusting something better is coming, and we start believing nothing *at all* is coming. An easier way to say this: take what you can get.

A good way to test the bullshittery of settling is to remember a time you thought nothing else would ever come along, and something did: another job, another apartment, another chance, another friendship, another pet, and yes, *another date*—another anything. If you've ever thought nothing else would ever come along and something did, you already have proof that this line of thinking is flawed. Fear of the future has a lot of absolutes in it, and honestly, I don't think that many of us are that psychic. We don't know the future, but we fear the worst anyway. I don't see why we can't choose to look forward to the best instead.

We tend to latch onto singlehood narratives that don't serve us. I don't blame us for that, I happen to think most of the singlehood narratives out there don't serve us and we can only consume what's floating around in the ether. If everything we absorb is a false or outdated narrative, and we don't see any other options, *that's* what we're going to believe about our own singlehood. Thank heavens we're allowed to find new narratives, eh?

The idea that whatever is in front of us right now is the last thing that will ever come along so we should take what we can get, is a negative, false narrative—and a common one. Here's another: something is better than nothing.

Have you heard that? Have you *lived* that? I have. The notion that something is better than nothing keeps us holding on to things we don't really want—or that aren't adding to our lives in a positive way. This is why we don't end bad relationships, and why we force ourselves to go on second dates with people we don't actually want to see again. We assume that something is better than nothing, that nothing else is ever coming, and that singlehood itself is also a version of nothing. If you've ever felt this way, it's okay—we're working on it.

Singlehood is not nothing. Your life, just because you live it as a single person, is not nothing. It does not lack anything to make it real. Your singlehood is as full and abundant as you choose to make it. And I encourage you to choose abundance! Building a full life for yourself is one of the ways you start to see the uselessness in settling. If your life is full of things like a career, friendships, hobbies, pets, travel, side hustles, family, community, philanthropy, learning, and *fun*, settling doesn't stand a chance! Settle? What the hell for?! Singlehood is a lot of things, but nothing isn't one of them.

This is really important to me: when I finally began to understand singlehood was not nothing, and I didn't have to settle, I calmed the hell down about "finding someone," forever. Suddenly, my singlehood was *better* than what was happening to me in the dating space. I wasn't "giving up;" I was snapping out of a terrible mindfuck. I'd let the pursuit of partnership, my aging body, the presumed unavailability of "good guys," the shame of being out in public alone, and so much more combine to terrify me into a dating culture dependency. The only thing that mattered to me was "finding someone," finding *anyone*, if it meant I could solve my singlehood problem. Now, I wake up every day grateful that I let go of that endless grind, that I never settled, and that I've realized why I don't have to. The relief I feel is a miracle.

You know something better than settling? This book. My podcast. My career. As soon as I deleted the dating apps and let go of a crazed need to "find someone," I received proof it was possible to live a happy single life, and I finally had time to follow some dreams. I also had a lot more headspace to be creative and grow, because I wasn't swiping my sanity away anymore. The two and a half years I've been app-free have been the happiest and most abundant of my life. I have so much more now than dating apps or dating culture ever gave me.

Fear of the future is a human feeling. It's almost a default setting, especially for women. Here's a good way to explain it:

Old thought: *I'm so scared of what's coming for me. I'm scared nothing good is coming for me.*
New thought: *I'm so excited to see what's next for me.*

We're scared because we think what's coming is bad or nothing. We're worried that if we don't settle, we won't have anything at all—or we'll have something even worse than the just-okay option in front of us.

I don't see our futures, or what's coming for us, as good *or* bad. I see every part of life as an education. Everything we experience in life contributes to who we are as people and how we develop into ourselves. I don't think that development ever stops. One of the ways I deal with the tougher days of my singlehood (they still happen!) is by trying to find the opportunity in them. What opportunity is a difficult time or shitty situation presenting to me? What am I meant to learn here?

A good example, and an easy reframe: Ghosting.

Old thought: *Why did he ghost me? Why doesn't he like me enough to continue interacting with me?*

New thought: *Thank goodness he showed me who he really is. I wouldn't want someone capable of that behavior, and I deserve better than that. Thanks for making it quick, Carl!*

Shifting from viewing the difficulties of singlehood as bad things happening to you, and into a space where you can look for opportunities to change your mindset, is such a massive and beneficial mental lift. I want you to give yourself credit and applause for even trying! Remember: we're working with a *lifetime* of old narratives here. There's not a lot of societal support for this sort of reframing, so I want you to be truly proud of yourself. This work is hard, and it can make us feel alone, but we're not alone—not even close. Feeling completely *done* with singlehood unhappiness and developing a desire for change is happening to *so many of us*.

Finding the opportunities, lessons, and gifts is not glossing over the negatives, by the way; it's not painting on false positivity. It's acknowledging something is happening that you'd prefer wasn't happening, and finding the opportunities to learn and grow anyway. It's about seeing value when and where we can, instead of seeing more and more problems to "deal with" and reasons to settle. I'm not asking you to flip everything around to make it shiny and happy and positive. I'm asking you to look for the lessons. This practice has certainly made me feel better, and I hope it helps you, too.

Fear of the future doesn't serve us as single women. That unknown—combined with the assumption that nothing good is coming, because nothing good is left, or whatever other lack messaging we're giving ourselves—is a lot! It's what motivates us to settle, to aggressively date when maybe we'd rather not, and to feel immense pressure to control something that isn't within our control. Fear of the future is a *doozy*.

It can take many forms, some which we've already talked about, including feeling "stuck" in situations like text-only relationships, or feeling like we can't ignore ghosts when they get back in touch. When we fear the future, we stay stuck and small, because that seems better than the uncertainty of the future we fear. Only it's not.

If you want to reframe fearing the future, take it a step at a time and practice. It's okay if it takes a little time to retrain your thought patterns. It's okay if this feels new. It isn't necessarily a quick fix, and I think you'll find that the quick fixes we've looked to in the past don't really work anyway.

Have you ever found yourself freshly ghosted, or recently appalled by someone's behavior on a dating app, and taken straight to social media to vent about it? That vent might make you feel better or more valid in the moment, because for some reason we feel better about shitty things happening to us when other people know they happened—but the feeling doesn't last. Venting creates a cycle of venting, because we're just bitching about the thing that happened. We're never looking deeper to ask ourselves why we feel bad about it, or what changes we can implement to feel better if it happens again in the future. We're also not asking what boundaries we can set to help prevent it from happening again.

It's of course perfectly okay to get upset when things go down in the singlehood and dating space that we don't like. Your feelings will always be valid, but I want you to know that what comes *after* those feelings can benefit you more than venting ever did. Make those shitty situations work for you! Someone has just invaded your day and your mental space with their gnarly behavior. You deserve to get something productive out of it.

I try to glean all the information I can from disappointing moments, to squeeze them for all their value, because I refuse to let them invade my space and leave me with nothing but a desire to vent in return. I will learn and grow from them; they will be gifts to me. Also, given my line of work, they're content. Between us chickens, my motto is: *May whatever hurts my feelings make me money.* Go ahead and ghost me, Steve—you're nothing but inspiration in a pair of dirty Vans.

I want to break this concept down into a really practical reframe, because I think getting into the habit of addressing these situations as they occur really helps us move past any impulse to settle.

For example, imagine this scenario: *Ugh! I just went on the best date ever—it was five hours long! I thought we both had a great time! So why isn't he texting me back?!*

This is one of those situations in the dating world that makes no goddamned sense. Maybe it would be fine if it happened to you once. You could chalk it up to whatever you wanted—he wasn't interested in you, he got busy, he was hit by a laundry truck—whatever. But when it happens over, and over, and *over* again, when something as confusing as an amazing first date that leads to literally nothing repeats itself, our thoughts can run away with us a bit. And I don't fucking blame them.

The thought process that can follow one of these scenarios might go a little something like this: *I'm being ghosted. I did something wrong. I do dating wrong. He doesn't like me. I'm not desirable.*

But what if we could switch the thought process following the exact same scenario to: *I'm so glad five hours was all I spent with someone capable of this ghosting behavior. What can I learn here? What is the opportunity? Let's see...I got some great practice meeting a new person and getting to know someone. And when I was ghosted, I was able to consider reframing it instead of spiraling—I'm proud of myself.*

You can take it even further, if you want! *What about this person's behavior makes me feel bad? Is it because I feel unwanted? Why do I want to feel wanted? Do I want to feel wanted by this guy specifically, or just any guy? Where does my need to feel wanted come from, and what is it telling me I need? How can I give myself what I need when that need isn't being fulfilled by someone else? How am I in charge of how I feel, rather than allowing someone else to be?*

And my personal favorite reframe: *Why does it always have to be the guy that determines where things go, or how things move forward? Why does it always feel like I'm the one sitting here hoping I don't get ghosted? I am in charge, too. I can decide how long my dates are, and being ghosted after a super long date felt terrible. So now I know I need to set boundaries around dates and limit them to shorter time frames, with the expectation that he can reach out to see me again if he'd like to spend more time together than the length of time I decide our first date will be.*

You are not limited to the same gut-reaction thoughts you've always had in the singlehood and dating world. You can choose new ones. You can choose to *stop* seeing things like ghosting or disappointing scenarios of any kind as just more examples of how much singlehood sucks or how unwanted you are. That change is allowed—and encouraged. Because singlehood *doesn't* suck, and the right people for you *will* want you. Maybe whatever shitty dating situation that just happened was providing the vital information that they're not it for you. Personally, I don't like mystery in dating—I like it when they make things clear. *Byeeeeeeee!*

Seeing the benefit to you in a situation, even a shitty one, makes it easier to move on. It also helps you avoid internalizing someone else's lack of manners as your own lack of desirability. Don't give a ghost that much power or credit. The ghosting behaviors of others and our own desirability aren't related. We aren't responsible for the bad manners other people choose. You didn't cause someone to ghost you any more than you caused someone to cut you off in traffic. Those behaviors say more about who *they* are than who *you* are.

Here's a big one: let's actually reframe fearing the future.

If our old thoughts are *I'm afraid of what's coming* or *I'm afraid that nothing good is coming*, we can see these fears from a few new angles:

- *The future isn't something I* have to *fear. The future is something I* get to *experience. I don't have to fear it; I get to look forward to it.*

- *Everything I experience is an opportunity to learn, grow, and find out who I want to be in the world. The future is giving me those opportunities.*

- *I am supporting my future self by not settling for less than what I want in the present.*

Whoever they are, they're not the last person you're ever going to match with. They're not the last person who's ever going to text you. This is not the last date you will ever go on. We don't have to know if or when we'll meet our future partners to decide that we don't have to settle for less than what we deserve right now. When you reframe the future as something to look forward to, rather than as something to fear, this process gets a whole lot easier.

We don't have to know everything. That space of not knowing doesn't have to be scary. It can involve a feeling of trust, too. The default setting of the unknown does not have to be a negative one. We don't have to know what the future holds. It's okay to let go and let what's coming, come. We can just allow it to unfold, because any energy spent worrying about it or trying to steer it a certain way is wasted when you realize that it's happening the way it's going to happen anyway—and it literally always has. You can choose to see the future as something that's bringing you nothing good, or as something that's affording you endless opportunity. It's your choice.

Our singleness, no matter at what age it happens to us or how long it lasts, can never diminish our inherent value as human beings. I don't care what messages we receive from society or how many sad head tilts at dinner we get from friends. Our value and validity as single people are identical to the value and validity of those in couples.

When we're out there in the world, you know, *not settling*, there's a lot of information to take in all the time. Our own beliefs come into play when we process that information. I'm a big fan of planning ahead in *many* areas of singlehood, but for now, let's just identify a few key settling areas.

That way, when they come up in the real world, it will be easier for us to recognize what's happening and reframe things for ourselves.

There are a lot of things we don't have to settle for in the singlehood space. Let's dive into a few of my favorites.

SCRAPS OF ATTENTION

One-word text responses. Responses containing nothing more than one emoji. An out-of-the-blue text six months after someone ghosted you. An Instagram like or a story view (fuckin' window-shoppers). Inviting you out, but only in group settings where they then don't speak to you all night and purposefully walk to the other side of the room every time you're near them (really happened to me!). Any little bread crumb of attention that keeps us following an endless trail through the woods. When we continue to stay invested in people who feed us scraps, we're settling.

You deserve someone who's excited that you texted them, someone who texts you back with coherent sentences or even (gasp!) responds by asking to see you. Or texts you *first*—imagine it! You deserve someone who doesn't leave you with little attention crumbs and tons of questions. You deserve someone with whom you always feel like you're on equal and firm footing. You don't have to settle by investing your energy, headspace, or heartspace in anyone less.

BAD BEHAVIOR

You don't deserve to be treated poorly, either online or in real life. You don't have to settle for mistreatment of any kind, and you are allowed to simply walk away from it. You don't have to leave with a proper goodbye, closure, or whatever else is trending right now. There's one exception where ghosting is okay: when they fired shots first. If someone treats you like shit, block them and forget them. Ghost. Ghost that ass.

LOWER LIFE STATUS

It's the old "single girls get the couch" routine. Nope! Single women do not have to settle for being viewed by their friends and family as "less than." We are not sitting at the kids' table at holidays. We are not sitting at the "leftover people" table at a wedding. We don't have to participate when someone asks us publicly, "Why are you still single?" We do *not* have to settle for being treated as less important, less valid, or less "adult in any scenario, ever, simply because we're single.

Not settling in these scenarios will definitely take some practice. It can feel a little uncomfortable at first to stay grounded in our self-worth and refuse to accept lesser versions of things, but as you keep practicing, it gets easier. You also learn that standing up for yourself and what you deserve won't make the world end. It might even help educate those around you, too.

ENTERTAINING OTHERS

Our single lives are not entertainment for other people. Our singleness and the experiences that come along with it are not here so that other people can have a voyeuristic little window into how the other half lives. We don't have to suffer through telling our stories just so someone else can remember how grateful they are to be married. Our single lives are not freely accessible to other people who want to sample singlehood just for a minute. If Jennifer wants to know what it's like to use a dating app, she can end her relationship and download one for herself. She doesn't have the right to flip through yours like it's a toy. Your life isn't her amusement.

WHATEVER WE CAN GET

You should have what you want, not what you settled for. You can believe your options are limited, or you can start to understand your singlehood is not a limitation. Taking "whatever we can get" is bottom-feeding our way through life. Who says we have to?

You lead your life—the outdated, narrow, shaming opinions of others are not in charge. Your singlehood is not a problem, and when it's not a problem, you don't feel compelled to fix it by settling for "whatever you can get, because something is better than nothing."

My singlehood isn't something that diminishes my market value by the day, insinuating I should settle. Remember that instead of seeing singlehood as punishment, misfortune, or lack of completion, we can choose to see it as protective instead. That way, we're not simply saying no to settling; we're saying yes to everything our lives have in store for us. I have a feeling there's much more to our lives than a constant search for someone else—and certainly more than a search that ends in settling.

New Year's Eve

I haven't used the word "alone" a lot. Personally, I don't believe single women are alone. I think we have far too many family members, friends, pets, and ways to occupy our time to ever *actually* be alone, and I don't value a romantic partner so far above any of my other company that it can wash away the benefits I get from having everyone else. However, alone happens. Alone can feel sad, scary, and lonely—that's valid. I am not above these feelings, I empathize with all of us going through them, and I don't want to leave you without offering some help.

Certain single moments are harder than others. We've all, at some point, known what it's like to feel alone, uncomfortable, and maybe even exposed at the same time. These are the moments that make us think, "Can I just fucking find someone already? Why do I have to do everything alone? Other people aren't alone, why am I?"

Often, something that's hard for one single person will be easy for another—it's all very personal. As this is a book *I'm* writing, we're going to talk about *my* hardest moment, in the hopes that it translates well to whatever moments are hardest for you. I enjoy glitter, champagne, and throwing parties at my house so that I don't have to go anywhere. So we're going to talk about being single on New Year's Eve. I'll toss in some general holiday stuff, too, just for grins.

It's a simple fact, proven by my Google Analytics data and seasonal DMs: it's harder to be single during the holidays. I can literally see it in the numbers, if I didn't already have firsthand experience with these annual difficulties myself. More people search "What if I never get married?" or "Why am I single?" during November and December, and I take a great deal of comfort and pride knowing that many times, my website is what they find. There's a lot of dating-driven garbage out there, and I love to offer counterpoints and support.

The holidays have a way of bringing people together, but what if you're a person who is already together? Someone whole and valid on their own, still deserving of wonderful holidays? What if you're someone who doesn't get to have the matching pajama photo moments, who isn't getting gifts from other people, and who isn't kissing someone at midnight? On top of all this, there's nothing like the holiday season to get people really oversharing on social media, showing off everything they have, and reflecting back to us everything that we don't. (Go read the chapter about comparison again if you need to; this is what it's there for.)

There's a level of unfairness that gets highlighted during the holidays. Even someone completely happy and content in singlehood can admit that. It's okay to feel confused, angry, jealous, or just like...left out. As always, though, I want us to really look at what's happening, and then reframe it. We get to feel better about things when we want to—that's allowed.

Remember how we got here: pretty much all of us were socialized into a society that groomed us to value couplehood and marriage over literally everything else. But that society had no way of knowing that when it came time for us to actually go out and get those things, the biggest tool at our disposal would be the cesspool that is dating apps. On top of that, society also had no way of knowing that ours would be the first generation to consume the happiness of others being boasted about in a constant stream via a little computer that we hold in our hands. Being single is harder at the holidays? No shit.

My whole thing, though: what if it wasn't?

What if being single didn't make us feel bad, and we didn't feel compelled to fix it at any cost? What if it were just another 100 percent valid and happy way to live, and a part of life that no one saw as a problem? What if we felt the confidence and validity to buy the goddamned pajamas for ourselves? (And our pets, obviously. This is no time for restraint. If you want to dress your plants up in red plaid, I'm here for it.)

The idea of a holiday, or any special time in life, being somehow "less" because we experience it alone isn't going to work for me. I think life's most epic moments don't have to burn less brightly for us just because we don't have "someone to share them with." Fuck that! I don't want being single to be something we "accept," "deal with," or "manage." I want more for us than just accepting our lives, as if they're somehow a consolation prize version when compared to the lives of couples. My life is not less simply because I don't have a romantic relationship. My life is the grand prize, the big trophy. The one so tall you need a ladder to dust it—that's my life, with or without someone else.

I want being single to be a time when we thrive. I want us to look forward to the holiday moments and traditions we create for ourselves and to look back on the holidays we spent single with fondness, rather than an overwhelming sense of relief that we're not single anymore. I don't want us to look back on the single part of our lives and have the prevailing thought be, "I'm glad that's over." Our singlehood is a whole lot more precious than something we just have to "get through."

Singlehood is too full of freedom, potential, and autonomy to wish it away as fast as possible. It's also potentially a decent chunk of time! I've been single for over thirteen years, and that's *way* too much of my life to have hated. It's also way too much time to hate holidays or avoid some of the sparkliest parts of life because I'm embarrassed to be alone.

I will never look back on my singlehood with disgust—more like pride and gratitude for everything I got to experience and learn. I don't mind telling you: I'm pretty sure I'll *miss* my solo holidays someday when I'm partnered.

But I didn't always feel this way. For a (very) long time, singlehood for me was just endless swiping into oblivion, never meeting anyone, and feeling like I was in a hell that I couldn't climb out of, no matter how hard I tried. My effort was never met with reward; in fact, I received quite a lot of punishment instead. I felt like I was losing my mind—*especially* at the holidays. Now I podcast and write about how fucking rad singlehood can be, so what I'm saying is: change is possible.

I realize that suddenly snapping out of single misery is asking a lot of a community programmed to be ashamed of singlehood since the moment their long-term memories came online, so let's be gentle with ourselves, shall we?

The way to feel better about being single, especially at the holidays, is to reframe the way you think about it. I know, shocking! By now, you're seeing how this stuff works. You allow yourself to view things from a different angle, and in broadening that lens for yourself, you lift your thoughts up to a more positive place. Those elevated thoughts then help you genuinely feel better about being single, too. And with more positive thoughts and emotions around being single, we are free to just *live* and stop treating every waking moment as an opportunity to hunt down a relationship. Can you ignore my advice as nonsense, double down on not wanting to be single anymore, and just continue swiping? Sure. But if you're really, deeply tired of that, why not give reframing a try?

With reframing, the exact same situation is taking place; we're just choosing to see it from an angle we haven't examined before. Let's try a few.

Old thought: *If I could just find someone, I'd be happy.*
New thought: *There is no perfect life situation that fixes all problems and has none of its own. I'm so lucky I have this time alone to figure out what really makes me happy, because another person will never be responsible for my happiness. That's my job.*

Old thought: *My friend just got engaged in front of the Christmas tree. I am so jealous. Why can't I meet someone and get engaged? What's wrong with me?*
New thought: *There is nothing inherently more "right" about my friend than me. She just happened to meet someone. I just haven't met someone yet. My singleness isn't a sign that I'm flawed. She didn't get engaged because she's perfect. Also, I'm so happy for her.*

Old thought: *I can't believe I'm spending another holiday alone.*
New thought: *I get to spend this holiday doing exactly what I want—or don't want. This holiday is entirely mine.*

Old thought: *I'm alone at the holidays this year, so I should just get a little mini tree.*
New thought: *I don't deserve something less or smaller just because I'm single.*

True story: I had a mini tree for *years*. (I was raised Jewish with zero Christmas trees, but in my adulthood I decided to start having a "Holiday Tree" because I like sparkly things, which is what I'm referring to here, but...semantics.) I actually thought a mini tree was all I was supposed to have. I'm just one person, so I don't get a full-size tree. I really thought that! It seems insane to me now, but back then, it was very much my reality. Then one year, while I was working at a job that treated me like *shiiiiiiiiit*, the art team was about to throw out a white, six-foot, faux Christmas tree. She was too beautiful for a dumpster. She was coming home with me. We hopped in a taxi from Manhattan to Brooklyn together and for six years now, she's been my tree. I cover her in little golden lights and, most years, nothing else at all. Accessorizing her with ornaments seems like putting lipstick on a marble bust. She's perfect just as she is.

Every year, the day I assemble her (which in my house is November 1—you're single, live how you want), I open a bottle of champagne, turn on the Spotify *Downton Abbey* Christmas mix (it's as good as you're hoping it is), and remember what I deserve. I deserve a full-size tree. I deserve to enjoy my holidays. I deserve to make them look and feel exactly as I believe they should. My days of a mini tree the size of a Shih Tzu on its hind legs are long gone.

You know how I said I'm going to miss my solo holidays someday? It took learning how to reframe my singlehood to teach me that even though I'll miss them, I'm allowed to bring my personal traditions with me into relationships. My future partner is welcome to join me in setting up Tree, but if he doesn't want to, that's fine! She and I have always enjoyed each other's company. If he'd like a tree that's green, or perhaps real, he's welcome to it! We can each bring the celebrations we love into the relationship. He's gonna clean up those needles, though.

Your singlehood isn't something that's wrong with you, and the only one who can really tell you that in a way that sticks is you. I'm just telling you it's an option; it's up to you to start seeing it that way. I suggest getting in some practice before the holidays.

So, New Year's Eve. How do we do it? Yes, I'm actually going to give you advice about my second-favorite holiday. (Halloween claims the number one spot.) I have a list of best practices that I think can help singles celebrate holidays in ways that feel exciting and fun. We deserve to look forward to these days, not just to survive them. Everything I'm about to tell you to do, I do myself. And every year, it really helps.

PLAN AHEAD

As we've discussed, I am a huge fan of advanced planning of all kinds, especially for single women. Disorganization and unpreparedness are the enemies of single holiday joy—you heard it here first. I know everyone is bad at planning New Year's Eve. No one likes this holiday (except me), because for some reason we associate it with high expectations but never take the time to prepare anything of the caliber we're expecting. So, yeah...New Year's Eve does suck when you expect it to wow you without putting in any effort first.

I've celebrated the holiday as a single person in every way you can imagine, and my all-time best piece of advice is this: wherever you're going, whatever you're doing, get there and stay there. Go to one place, and don't leave until you go home. Bar hopping on New Year's Eve is a one-way ticket to crying on a sidewalk. We can do better.

A few of my favorite NYE ideas: pre-dinner drinks at a friend's house or yours, whoever's within *walking* distance of your chosen restaurant (mandatory, or skip the pre-game), followed by a 9 p.m.-ish seating at that restaurant, and hopefully it's doing a *prix fixe* menu. Around eleven or so, the staff will start reveling along with you, and by the stroke of midnight, everyone is lighting sparklers and having a great time. Take a cab or car service straight home from there. You can also go to a big-ticket party or ball of some kind if that's your thing; just make sure you really like the friends you're going with or that you know a lot of people there. Alone in a big room full of strangers is no way to ring in a new year. Trust me—I've done it. House parties are one of my strongest recommendations, either at your house or someone else's. Feeling comfortable, welcome, and safe as you welcome in a new year is a good vibe.

I also enjoy treating myself to an evening at a hotel on New Year's. This is one you use when you're going to be totally on your own that night, because it's something that feels really special and celebratory, even by yourself. This is what I did during the pandemic New Year's, and I had an amazing time. I brought my own snacks and supplies, a sparkly top, and had many, many little photoshoots in my ridiculously chic hotel room.

The key is, plan ahead. Your outfit, your menu, your playlists, anything you want or even *think* you'll want for that night, or even the day after—get it together in advance. Moments when you feel untethered and don't know what to do can exacerbate difficult emotions that come up around singlehood and the holidays. When you plan in advance, you set yourself on firm footing. Failing to do even a little bit of planning ahead has the potential to leave you sad and frustrated, and you're too cute for that. What feels "special" will vary from person to person, and I encourage you to tailor your evening specifically to you. That's allowed.

FUCKIN' GLITTER!

This is no time for neutral tones. Things that glitter and sparkle really do lift the mood, and we have Christmas to thank for leaving a lot of that shit lying around for us by New Year's. Lights, sparkles, sequins, edible glitter if you've got it—I don't care. Confetti is confetti, no matter how many people are vacuuming it up the next day—and honestly, unless you have shag carpeting, it's really not that big of a deal. The point is, just because you're celebrating single doesn't mean you're not "enough" to celebrate fully. I want to wake up with sparkles in my sheets the next morning—do you hear me?

We live in a culture that centers people in couples and families, as if people who are alone are somehow less worthy of living life fully. Not this time, dammit—not on *our* New Year's Eve. Yes, that entire cheese plate is for you. Yes, that entire bottle of champagne or nonalcoholic sparkling beverage is yours. Yes it's "just you." Who the fuck cares? Honestly if anyone cares, gives you side-eye, or makes you feel ashamed for throwing yourself a *real* New Year's Eve, they don't need to remain in your life after midnight. There's a resolution for you.

MANAGE MIDNIGHT

The stroke of midnight can be difficult as a single person in a room full of people who have a designated person to kiss. This is a tough one; I won't lie to you. I've struggled with it for years, and there are times it still feels difficult. My strategy? Alternative activities! As the ball drops, I like to position myself in a place with a good photographic vantage point, perhaps on top of a chair, and designate myself the historian of the group, snapping photos of the countdown and the midnight kisses, both of which usually delight the crowd. This gives me something to do when everyone else is kissing, and I don't feel left out at all. Also, single people get *all* the hugs and kisses immediately after everyone kisses their partner, which is really nice. You can also designate yourself the DJ or champagne and sparkler distributor, or you can go outside on the balcony by yourself and listen to everyone in the neighborhood doing countdowns of their own. There are options other than standing there watching everyone else kiss at midnight—pick one.

BE SAD IF YOU WANT!

Shining on fake positivity is not what I'm about. If you're sad, be it. Be everything you authentically are. It's all okay. It's all allowed. Crying is fine. It's more than fine—it's healthy and cathartic and healing. Resist the urge to resist the urge to cry, is what I'm saying. Whatever you're feeling on your New Year's—or birthday, or Hanukkah, or the Fourth of July—is exactly what you're allowed to feel. There might be a compulsion to "fix" what you're feeling or make yourself feel a different way, as if feelings of sadness were ill-timed on New Year's Eve. But the way someone living through modern singlehood is feeling, whenever they're feeling it, is always right on time.

DISTRACT, DISTRACT, DISTRACT

Sometimes, when things are too much, my brain and my nervous system simply need a break. Distractions and things that occupy my mind so much that it shuts off entirely are exactly the break I need. Again, these will be unique to the individual, and I always find that movies do the trick, perhaps even stand-up comedy specials—I've also been known to go apeshit on old episodes of *The West Wing*. Cooking is a great way to distract myself, but I don't want to get anything on my sparkly top. Perhaps you enjoy a good dance party or spin class? There are no wrong answers. I create a diversion for my brain so that I can take things a little easier when I need to. I usually plan ahead (see?) and save a really fun and special distraction for myself on New Year's Eve or New Year's Day. I go into any holiday with a few coping skills in place, and I'd suggest you do the same. If it turns out you don't need them, save them for next time!

LEVERAGE TECHNOLOGY

Another smart coping mechanism that grew out of what we all lived through in 2020 is connecting with friends and family anywhere in the world via Zoom, FaceTime, Skype, and the like. In my opinion, these tools have broadened our options for friendships from where we live to literally *all the places people live.* Book a distanced party with friends in other countries and use their countdowns if you don't think you can stay awake long enough to see yours. (Unless you live in one of the first places where midnight happens, in which case just do your best.) Catch up with old friends from out of town while you decorate or new friends you met in a Facebook community while you put on your *glitter.* Join two long-distance house parties together via the magic of the internet. Hell, project a Google Meet onto a wall and double the size of your guest list without having to buy extra snacks. Get creative! We have far more options than just waiting for someone to invite us somewhere, okay?

NO PRESSURE

You really don't have to do anything. If it feels like too much, then it is. New Year's Eve or any other holiday is allowed to be just another night to cook dinner, watch a couple of episodes of your show, and then go to bed. You're not letting anybody down here—permission granted. New Year's Eve can smell pressure, and it's perfectly okay to release yourself from any obligation you feel around this holiday or any other.

Remember how much your life belongs to you and no one else. Explaining yourself to others and explaining why you're choosing to celebrate—or not—in a certain way is never required. You never have to satisfy anyone else's curiosity with an explanation or justification as to why you make your choices. Fuck 'em.

No holiday pressure is required any year, but most certainly during your single years. It's okay to let it all go. You don't have to feel like you missed an opportunity, either! Remember, January 1 is a day on a calendar. Your own personal "fresh start" can begin whenever you want, or as many times as you want. May 7 is a nice day. So is August 4. November 15? Glorious. The year is yours—do whatever you want with it.

LOOK FORWARD

Forget resolutions or intentions or whatever Instagram tries to tell you turns you into a "goddess" or some shit.

Remember what it feels like to look forward to things. And when that's hard, take an accounting of everything you have to feel happy about and grateful for right now—cheesy, but mentally effective, I promise you. I find when things are hard, and have been hard, remembering everything I learned and everything I made it through makes me feel proud. I remember that we get to *be here*, and what a lucky concept that is in the first place. Looking forward and having hopes for the future are allowed, maybe most especially when you're single.

The holidays don't have to be a time of unhappiness for us. They're truly my favorite time of year, full of personal traditions and decor and really, really cute sleepwear. Honestly, I think it would be such a shame for me to look at all I have, to look at this time of my life that I'm able to completely customize, and still only focus on one thing I don't have—a partner.

I wish more than just acceptance of our single status for this community. I wish genuine happiness, too. Because when we have that, it becomes so much less likely that we'll leave our singlehood behind for anyone who's less than deserving of our time and love. For now, we are here, living our lives and celebrating them in any way we see fit. We truly do have an endless capacity to live life fully and to enjoy it, and when I see that capacity diminished by old narratives around singlehood, it makes me want to work even harder to help. I have too much love and respect for singles to let us live lesser lives simply because of our single status—every day, but especially on the big days.

Remember my mini tree. She was cute, and she was festive, but only minimally so. A tiny tree was telling me I only deserved a tiny holiday, or a *little bit* of fun and joy. The only reason I thought I deserved less than what other people had in their homes was that I was single. I thought that meant I had to have everything in single-serving size—even fun. If I can come out of that headspace and into a mindset where my singlehood isn't something to apologize for, but rather something that makes my life even more special and customized to me, I promise you anyone can.

Fully living in happy singlehood is not an impossible task. Some days will be harder than others, and a lot of those days will be "important" ones. Days are allowed to be hard, and holidays are allowed to be sad. But they aren't required to be simply because we're single. I think coming to a place where we understand the difference, and start living like it, is worth celebrating.

1 6

You Will Not Be Single Forever

Don't tell anyone, but sometimes I think we hate singlehood because we want to—because we're afraid anything other than disgust with our singlehood, anything other than a constant effort to end it, will result in being single forever. And we've been programmed to think being single forever is the worst thing in the world.

I think we choose to hate being single because we believe if we don't, we'll get even more singlehood in return. As if enjoying singlehood somehow communicates to the Universe that we don't want a partner. Instead of choosing reframing and happiness, we choose an unhappy singlehood grind, because we think *that's* what will ensure we find a relationship. If this doesn't sound logical to you, good. You're learning how many singlehood beliefs are full of shit. Let's reframe them. I love you.

To my great regret, I don't have a magic crystal that I can gaze into and tell you precisely when and where to meet your partner. No one has this, but plenty of people will try to sell you on "fixes" to your singlehood all the same. When I say, "You will not be single forever," I do mean it, but it's not based on any sort of ability to see the future. Instead, it's based on what I've experienced in the past.

First, if you want it, I think you deserve a partnership. You're a living being on this earth, and that alone makes you worthy of being here, thriving here, and certainly finding someone to hold hands with here. I don't think our singlehood, at whatever age and for however long, makes us less worthy of finding the thing that will make us not single anymore. We certainly don't deserve it less than anyone else who already found it.

People in couples aren't in couples because they're perfect or somehow more deserving than you. Lucky that they found something they wanted? Maybe. But more deserving of it than you? Never. I've never looked at a friend of mine who was single and then met someone and thought to myself, "It's because she deserves it more than me." I've also never looked at the person a friend met and thought, "Dammit, that's exactly the one I want—I can't believe she got there first." We are deserving, our timing is unique to us, and the right people for us are unique to us, too.

Next, logic tells me we're going to partner if we want to. Pretty much everyone I've ever known already has. Couplehood isn't an anomaly; it's what pretty much everyone does, unless you're someone who prefers singlehood and specifically chooses it. The frequency with which people have relationships tells me that the odds alone are in our favor. We're not asking for something insane here. We're asking to do something that countless millions around the world are already doing. Honestly, y'all, I don't think we're that weird. If we want to partner, I believe we will.

I have to stress the idea that we won't be single forever and give you my reasons for believing it's true, because I really do think there's a false belief attached to hating singlehood. We think our hatred of singlehood and the misery that comes along with it will somehow lead us to love one day. We're afraid to stop hating singlehood because we think it will keep us single forever—as if loving and appreciating something that we *also* want to change at some point were the same as telling the Universe to keep the love of our lives to itself. It's nonsensical to me. I understand why we believe it, and I believed it for a decade, but it's nonsense to me all the same. We are allowed to love this single life and still remain open to and desirous of relationships at the same time. We don't have to choose one or the other. Ever.

I'm much more comfortable in my belief that loving this life and living it happily will eventually lead to partnership, as opposed to clinging to a shame-filled, miserable existence where I hate my singlehood and somehow think living unhappily will make singlehood end faster. I think love wins out over hate every time, including when applied to single life before partnership.

I won't ask you to stop wanting partnership. I think partnership is fantastic, and I want it, too! But maybe we can work a little bit on this fear of permanent singlehood. Not so we can choose permanent singlehood, but so we can live happier lives, less burdened by a constant singlehood "problem." I haven't asked you to choose, accept, or embrace your singlehood once in this book, and I don't intend to start now. Those are very different moods from the one I wish for single women. I don't think our singlehood is something we have to choose forever in order to be happy. I don't like "accepting" or "embracing" singlehood, because those terms imply it was wrong to begin with. I think we deserve to do a lot more with our lives than just accept them.

Singlehood isn't a problem to me any more than a relationship is a solution. I think both singlehood and relationships are equal. I think they're equally valid ways to live and one isn't better than the other—but I've also lived in our society for almost four decades, and I understand how deep our preference for couplehood can go. I also know how it can prompt us to feel and what it can lead us to do. My hope is to help alleviate the pain that can come with an unhappy single life and to shine light on what's real and good about singlehood. The myths keep us miserable, while the truth is a relief. It would be amazing if we could try facing some of our singlehood fears, instead of trying to date our way out of them.

What if we *are* single forever? Can I ask? Previously, this has been a question too terrifying to ever explore, but as you may have noticed, I'm not scared of this shit. I'm far more afraid single women will keep swiping their lives away, taking in immeasurable amounts of disappointment and emotional harm the whole time—all while ignoring how *fantastic* it can feel to be single. I'm not afraid of us being single forever. I'm afraid of us finding a relationship and *then* realizing how great it was to be single.

I'm really asking: what if we are single forever? I operate on the assumption that when we fast forward to the end, it isn't as terrifying as we assume. Also, shedding light on our fears can help us feel less like they're coming to get us—at least that's been my experience.

What's waiting at the end of "forever?" Is that what we're worried about, dying alone? "Dying alone" is an idea that encompasses a lot more than just the last moments of our lives. It's intended to breed fear into single women, as if never partnering were the worst possible fate that could befall us. Anyone who uses dying alone as a threat has never spent a moment of their lives keeping someone company in a nursing home, of that I'm certain. If you fear "dying alone," you don't know what old age and dying really look like, and I think it's going to shock the shit out of you when you get there. I have news for you: the only way not to die alone is to die first.

I don't want to spend my entire life in service of the very end of it. I'd rather spend my time in the present, fully living, rather than just trying to get married at any cost so that in the last moments I have someone romantically committed to me in the room. Is that what we *really* care about? I don't think so. I don't think we care about the end half as much as we care about all the years in the meantime. "Dying alone" is a phrase we assign to *living* our entire lives alone, which is simply bad writing.

Telling someone to date themselves into a hellhole so that they don't "die alone" is nothing short of cruel. *Hey, you'd better force yourself to suffer through something unpleasant for as long as it takes so that in the very last minutes of your life, there's someone holding your hand.* It's such bullshit. We are up against *so much* that pushes women deeper and deeper into seeking solutions to something that isn't even wrong. Such advice shows a lack of respect, and to me, telling someone they should try not to "die alone" is incredibly dismissive of what single life is actually like for those of us living it.

Fuck how we die—how do you want to *live*?

What's waiting for you in an entire life lived alone? I'm on thirteen years now and feel like I've got a decent window into the situation, so let's evaluate! Work, friendship, family of origin, family of choice, travel, pets, homes, hobbies, skills, experiences, communities, self-discovery, and an entire life of being able to starfish in bed—I'm massively generalizing, of course, but I invite you to think about what your whole life would be full of if you lived it alone. Not what it would lack—what it would be *filled with*. I know it feels scary at first, but that's just our training. Opening up the aperture we're using to look ahead, and letting more of life into the picture, can rewrite the idea that a life lived alone is an empty one. I hope if we do live the rest of our days single, we won't spend all that time simply focusing on *one thing* we don't have. I genuinely have better things to do with my time.

Single life is an invitation to see *everything*, not to zero in on one thing only. Because I'll tell you this plainly: if you spend your singlehood only focusing on finding a relationship, once you're in one, the relationship will still be the only thing you focus on. Relationships where one person has *nothing else going on* other than the relationship itself are short-lived.

Before you read the next paragraph, know that I don't say this to accuse—I say it with love. I've done it *all*, too.

Sometimes I think we want to partner because of all the little extras that come with it. I think we've prized the things we "get" when we find a relationship because we've seen other people get them and show them off, and we're tired of being left out. Engagement rings are status symbols, and we want them. Weddings are a chance to be celebrated in a way society deems valid, and we want that, too. We want someone to go places with so that we don't feel ashamed about being places alone. We want the invasive questions about our singlehood to stop. We want to be able to say we're married and post shit on social media. Ignoring the fact that these things can actually matter to singles doesn't help us much. It's fine if they matter. I see no shame in any of this. My concern only comes in when the bells and whistles of relationships become the driving force in pursuing one.

The bells and whistles exist, for sure, but they exist in equal measure with the realities of couplehood, too. Compromise, sharing finances, merging into a new family, adding someone to *your* family, sharing a living space, accommodating preferences, disagreements, *big* disagreements, feelings of monotony—and that's just on normal days. There are sometimes big lows and even big highs that can jostle relationships in ways you don't hear about over drinks. Choosing to live your actual life together with another person is a big goddamn deal.

There's something in between the sparkles of couplehood and its less awesome realities. There's home. There's genuine respect and partnership and deep love. There's humor and company and friendship. There's peace and comfort, and I wish these things for all of us who want them. It is my belief, based on what I've seen in the world, that we'll have relationships at some point. Maybe not on the societal timeline, maybe not right when we want them, but maybe instead when they're actually right for us. A customized life timeline is no reason to resent your singlehood—because we can't see the future, and sometimes we can't even see how the present protects us or does us good. Being single right now is allowed to be a *good* thing, even if we don't find out why until later.

Call me crazy, but I don't think we can date so determinedly that we somehow force the right relationships into our lives. I really don't think that's how it happens. The right relationships come into our lives in an infinite number of ways, and at varying times. We're not all issued our ideal partner at twenty-seven years old. So maybe we're allowed to shed any shame around not meeting that artificial deadline, because maybe we're not meant to.

Companionship, love, sex, joy—these are all wonderful things. I'm not denying that. But a romantic relationship isn't the only place to find them, so sometimes I wonder what we're really after. I wonder why the pursuit of a romantic relationship is so intense, and I wonder why we believe the payoff is such a prize. I need other parts of life to matter more and relationships to matter a little less. I'm looking for more balance in the world, because once I found it for myself, I felt better. That balance helped me stop seeking societal approval through partnership, too. Just saying.

Once I stopped hating my singlehood, I had space to think about what the right relationships for me might feel like. It's counterintuitive, but I didn't know what I was really looking for until I stopped searching.

The world gets far too many things about singlehood entirely backward. In shining light on what we're truly afraid of, and what we're actually looking for, we can tell more truth and have less fear. I don't think you or I will die alone. I don't think we'll live alone, either. I don't think we're living alone right now.

When it comes to your singlehood, you have a choice. You can choose to see it as a problem, or you can choose to see it as a gift. Our thoughts aren't just things happening to us; we are actually in charge of them. We can decide how to think, and we can choose how we view the situations we find ourselves in.

Thoughts can change—I know this because for ten years, I thought my singlehood was what made me a lesser person than everyone I knew in a couple, and those thoughts made me *treat myself* as a lesser person, too. Today, I see and feel all the value in my singlehood and treasure it. My singlehood has educated me and given me space to become who I was meant to be, without diverting any of my attention to another person. I wouldn't know who I wanted to be in future relationships if I hadn't been lucky enough to spend this time single. So I probably would have just continued to twist myself into who I thought other people wanted me to be instead. And one by one, those relationships would end when my unhappiness boiled over and I assumed it was the relationship causing it. A relationship wasn't making me unhappy. My lack of knowledge about what I actually wanted in a relationship, other than it simply existing, plus my inability to be myself for fear of losing a relationship— that was the unhappiness. That's what I needed to work on, not my singlehood itself.

After reframing my thoughts about being single, there's no chance in hell of losing myself again. I will no longer change myself for the sake of keeping a relationship. I will instead acknowledge the relationship itself needs to change, and if it can't, it will end. Since I'm not afraid to be single anymore, being single sounds better than being in a relationship that's not right for me. In the ten years I hated my singlehood and did nothing more than try to swipe my way out of it, I had no idea about any of this. It took a *lot* of time, certainly—but it was worth it. My singlehood is not a problem but a blessing. That thought is effortless for me now. If this book can help even one person make a similar shift in thought patterns for themselves, it accomplished its goal.

Let me be quite clear: there isn't some magical choice you can make that will affect the outcome of your singlehood or your dating efforts. I'll never tell you to "think positive" so that you can find someone. I will, however, tell you there are countless benefits to reframing singlehood so that you no longer view it as something wrong or something you have to fix no matter what it takes—or how much the effort harms you. Changing the way you think about being single doesn't help you find a relationship; it helps you love every day of your life. It also helps you rethink which outcome is the greater prize.

I think hating singlehood keeps women frozen—in dating app hell and in bad relationships, because we think something is better than nothing. Singlehood is not nothing, and dating apps don't care about you. This isn't about thinking positively. It's about thinking for yourself.

In my experience, single women make too many choices in service of "finding someone." The old "If I do this, *then* I'll find someone" thought pattern. I've been criticized for my approach to dating. It's been suggested that in choosing to just live my life and allow the right relationships to show up whenever they show up, I'm too relaxed, not doing enough, or living in a fantasy. I always find it funny that *I'm* the one living in a fantasy, while there are still singles out there (and plenty of advice-givers) who think there's some magical alteration they can make to themselves and the way they date that will cause their partner to materialize in front of them. Who's living in a fantasy, really?

Beyond choosing to see singlehood as a problem, maybe we've also chosen to see it as unsolvable. How many times have you told yourself, "There are no good guys left," or something similar? How many lack-driven thoughts are in your head right now, and how many have you said out loud to a friend over dinner?

"I'll never find someone."

"There's no one left."

"It's the same guys on every app." (Yes, it is—delete them.)

How do you know that the situation is really as impossible as it seems in your mind? Are you psychic, all-seeing, all-knowing? Or are you just making grand assumptions driven by a difficult dating experience and a hatred of singlehood? Our experiences so far do not indicate the only things we will *ever* experience. That's not magic; it's logic. I hate toxic positivity and forced optimism, and that's not what I'm suggesting you try here. I'm suggesting you pay more attention to the reality of the situation and to the fact that you don't know everything—that's good news! There are 7.6 billion people on our planet. You can choose to assume you'll never, ever find someone, or you can rethink all the reasons why you're so intensely focused on looking.

I can never promise you that changing the way you think about being single will lead to you meet your partner. But I can promise reframing the way you think about being single can lead you to feeling better overall. If I had to choose satisfaction with my own life or a partner (I don't have to make this choice by the way—I can have both), I'd choose to love my life every time.

There's no magic here. Believe me: there's no one who wants magic to be real more than I do, but I will be the first one to tell you that singlehood is a realm where sorcery does not apply. You cannot "think positive" and make your partner appear. You cannot vision board him into existence. Your assumptions about what's out there aren't predicting the truth. Reframing singlehood for ourselves is practical, logical, and real—but it gets to *feel* magical, too.

When does "forever" start? What counts as being alone "forever?" It's one of life's little convenient words whose meaning shifts depending on the speaker's intention in the moment. Anything can feel like "forever" to anyone. Forever isn't real; it's relative. I'm thirty-nine years old, and I've been single for thirteen years. Have I been single forever yet?

Or does forever just mean you're single past the point that society celebrates you as a woman? Once you age into a space where women are no longer as desired for their youthfulness, beauty, or ability to procreate as they once were, does that mean you've been single for a woman's "forever?" I wonder what a man's forever is.

If you don't want to be single, I don't think you'll be single forever. I don't think I will be single forever. I think we're going to live our lives, and at some point during those lives, we're going to meet people with whom we can have beautiful partnerships that add to our experiences in positive ways. I think that's just part of how living goes.

In my opinion, our efforts in the dating space never have to result in a reward. If I tried, very actively, to find someone for a decade and didn't find *anyone*, experience tells me that I have just as much chance of meeting someone when I'm not putting *any* focus on dating as when it was all I could think about. Not centering my life around "finding someone" feels a lot better than dating ever did. It also leaves me with more time to do things I enjoy rather than consuming, and contorting, every free moment in attempts to meet someone. I haven't "sworn off" dating. I've made a conscious choice to stop letting it consume my life.

I have no idea when I'm going to meet someone, but I no longer care the way I used to, because I've seen the value of my single time. How long you're single doesn't matter when you're happy. That, my loves, is the point.

If the thing that's keeping you from letting go, from reframing the beliefs in your mind about singlehood for the better, is the notion that enjoying single life somehow signs you up for singlehood forever, it's time to take a deep breath. It's time to broaden your thoughts about singlehood and what it means to not have a partner—to see everything that's possible for us right now, rather than to *only* see one thing we don't have. I think the reality of being single is a lot less scary than the beliefs we've held in our minds. Singlehood is too amazing and full of possibility to spend it worrying we'll be that way forever. It's hard to worry about being something forever when it's awesome.

1 7

Free

Being single has a good side. It isn't talked about much, because the general assumption about singlehood is it's a problem that's somehow your fault. If you're single, the world assumes there's something wrong with you—wrong because you're probably causing your own singleness, and wrong simply because being single itself is wrong. Just because we've been calling out this bullshit for sixteen chapters now doesn't mean we're not still dealing with it every day in real life.

When someone finds out I'm single, they don't smile or congratulate me. Nobody's like *"Oooh, fun!* Tell me all about it!" I get more of the downturned mouth, the head tilt, the unrequested advice or words-of-comfort sort of response. I'm told not to worry because they're sure

I'll "find someone," even though I hadn't expressed concern about that. You probably know this vibe best as pity. Coupled people tend to pity single people, and if you press them on it, they'll never be honest with you. They'll never tell you what they really think is so bad about singlehood. All they'll say is, "We just want you to be happy."

The pity thing is confusing, when I think about all that singlehood affords me. I still have meeting my partner to look forward to—I still have those early, exciting days ahead. I think people forget that. They forget there are some pretty intriguing unknowns that I still have coming my way. They forget how nice a quiet house can be, or how much more likely it is there will be one seat open for dinner at the bar, instead of two. I'm pretty sure they can't remember a time when they could be 100 percent selfish without consequences. If they could, I don't think they'd feel so bad for me.

We're so timid about it, aren't we? As a society we don't dare put singlehood on a pedestal, because then what would that say about couples? Are we saying that—*gasp*—couplehood isn't the ultimate achievement?! I've reached a point in my life where I genuinely don't care what my happy singlehood says to the couples that observe it, but we still have to operate in a world that believes couplehood is better than singlehood, until you lift—forgive me—the veil. I'd rather tell the truth about the good side of being single, and if that makes someone doubt their partnership, so be it. Partnered people have been making me feel lesser because of my singlehood for a long time. I think I'm entitled to hit one back over the net.

The biggest, brightest reason to value singlehood and breathe in every delicious moment of it before it's gone is freedom, no question. Freedom is hard to pity, which makes me think people who pity singles have never really felt this kind of freedom. So actually, I pity *them*. I know they say ignorance is bliss but...so is never having to share your fries.

In our society, we've been so groomed to see single as a bad thing, something we need to date to the brink of madness in order to fix, that there often isn't room to stop and ask a really basic, essential question:

What's really so bad about being single?

We've just taken the presumed badness as truth, like when our parents told us to eat carrots so we could see in the dark. It's nothing more than a fiction spun to achieve the desired result. I eat carrots all the time, and my glasses are still as thick as the dictionary.

We live inside a Labyrinth (my favorite film, by the way) that draws us further and further toward the center, toward coupledom. And while there are perils and traps and dick pics strewn throughout, the maze itself is utterly magnificent. Being single is actually magnificent. But we rarely stop to notice its majestic beauty and wondrous secrets, and why would we? We think we're on a quest that ends in something even better. The opposite of single is supposedly love, and why waste time enjoying being single when you could put effort into finding love instead? Single bad. Love good. *Ludo down.*

We're overdue for an inventory of the good stuff—that's all. Reframing how we feel about our singlehood will be a lot harder if we can't see the wonderful parts of our situation first. We don't have to hate what we are, certainly not when there are so many fun perks to it. They're not even perks! They're just *how things are* when you're single. If you think about it, I bet you'll find a lot more to like than what you'd noticed before.

Your list will be different, of course, and if you'd like to tweet it to me *@shanisilver*, I'd really enjoy that, but here are a few of my favorite things about being single:

I always get the good cinnamon roll.

My choice of pet never has to accommodate anyone's allergy.

I haven't waited to watch the next episode of *anything* since the mid-2000s.

I don't have a "side" of the bed. I have the bed. The firmness of the mattress is also to my liking alone.

I never step on cold loose change. (This is specific to a former relationship of mine—for some reason, he always had a shitload of coins, always dropped them everywhere, and never picked them up.)

I've never had to give away clothes or shove all my shit to one side to make room for someone else's belongings.

I can wake up as early as I want and make whatever noise I want. I never have to tiptoe around my own damned house lest I wake someone up.

Dinner is a one-person decision.

I never have to explain myself. I never have to walk someone through why I do things or prefer things a certain way. I can just exist in peace. Everything is done my way, and my way isn't weird to anyone else. I like that.

There are many, many more positives, obviously, but you get the point. It's important to see the good that's right in front of us. The good stuff provides balance in a world that reiterates to us, at every opportunity, just how sad and wrong and lacking singlehood is. Taking stock of the good stuff helps you feel a lot more confident when you're out there in a world that treats you with pity.

I don't think seeing the good parts of being single is making the best of things, by the way. I'm not patronizing myself in identifying the little morsels of singlehood that make me happy. "Oh, look, Shani—here's something kind of nice. You can have that." No. I like my single life and all of its moving parts a *lot*, and I refuse to look at the way I live life and find it lower in status than coupled humanity. When you look around at all the freedom I have, this life is pretty top-shelf.

You know I respect couplehood, and I look forward to it for myself. I don't need couples to be miserable in order to see value in my single life. But there are times when I look at married people with an explosive sigh of relief. It's not unlike the feeling you get when you unzip high-waist pants. Every now and then...I kind of feel like we escaped. Like those of us single well into our adulthood have slipped out the back door of the Couplehood Compromise Palace, and nobody ever noticed.

Like when you see a woman pause before doing something because she has to discuss it with her partner first? That makes me want to vomit into the nearest vessel. I'm sorry, what? Are you about to get...*permission* right now?

Lauren, we're in our thirties. Or when someone sees an apartment they want to rent, or a dog they want to adopt, and they can't just...do it. They have to talk to *someone else first*—and there are countless moments like that in couplehood that are currently *not* a pain in my ass.

I get it. As part of a partnership, you check in with your partner first—for the trust factor, the strength of the relationship, and just plain old respect. Talking to each other and greenlighting big decisions for one another isn't controlling; it's textbook. It just isn't a textbook I have to lug around in my bag right now.

When you're single, it's totally normal (and sometimes alternativeless) to do things alone. Once you're partnered, there are assumed truths. Couples attend events together. Couples travel places together. Couples spend holidays together at whoever's family's turn it is. They eat dinner together at the same restaurant. They make fewer independent decisions and more compromises and assumptions. It's not bad; it's just true.

For me, my happiness in my single status really comes down to decision-making. What drives my decisions? I do, 100 percent of the time. If I have a desire, a curiosity, a need, even a whim, I am the guiding force behind it. Anyone who's decided to partner made one big decision that changed how *all other decisions* would be made for a very long time.

Also, I go to Paris. Every year, finances permitting, I take a trip to Paris alone. I stay in a tiny room in a boutique hotel with cute sconces and headboards and an elevator so small my suitcase and I require two separate trips. I get up at the crack of dawn to walk Parc Monceau and the Marché Bastille and all the other delightful sites that are open before 10 a.m. I don't fuss about with breakfast (usually a pastry and coffee will suffice) but book reservations for lunch and dinner, every day, precisely where I want to go. (Sometimes, I go to the same place twice!) I waltz through museums at my unique pace, focusing only on the art and eras that delight me the most, and I spend *hours* in museum gift shops. I waste no time, intricately planning my days with contingencies built in for the inevitable unpredictability of Parisian business hours or the occasional instance of tired feet. I am an organized, efficient, and highly exploratory traveler, to what would be considered a fault if I had any kind of company around to notice. But I don't, so my lists and maps and itineraries and I set out for adventure and have a great time.

I never have to "run it by" anybody or justify the destination in the face of, "But we went there last year." I know I went last year, I liked it last year, and I'm going to like it again this year, too. I'll never give up Paris. I'll always go, and I'll always go alone, because the value to me in a solo trip to Paris is part of what I discovered as a single person. Solo trips to Paris will always be part of my life, whether I'm single or partnered. He's welcome to meet me in Vienna in a week.

The time I've spent taking inventory of and embracing single life for the freedom it affords me has illuminated my self-worth. That self-worth was hiding behind the negativity societally associated with being single. In allowing myself to stop and assess what it really means to be single, I've improved my own opinion of what it means to be me.

There isn't anything wrong with me because I'm single. Instead, single has become a precious time in my life, full of unique experiences, exploration, and yeah, some selfish stuff, too. More than anything, though, I'm free. I'm free to do what I want, how I want, where I want, never pausing to get someone else on board, never accommodating what another person would rather do. The only thing that's better than being a mature and capable adult who's good at compromising is never having to compromise in the first fucking place. Married people get to have companionship, split rent, and have sex with someone they love and trust on a regular basis. I get this.

If seeing the good side of single has taught me anything, it's that if I'm going to give this kind of freedom up, whoever he is, he's going to have to be amazing to convince me to do so. And when you think about it, he should be. I don't have to settle for a relationship that's simply there, just so it can save me from singlehood. Because I don't need to be saved from something I love. I should only leave my singlehood when a partnership is right for me. That's the only relationship I'll ever be willing to leave singlehood for.

Would I know all this if I hadn't invested in the freedom of singlehood—if I hadn't really looked at single life and wondered, "Wait, why do I hate this again?" I doubt it.

What if the secret to a good relationship is to stop being scared of being single?

If we were less scared to be single, would bad relationships even exist? If we weren't afraid of being alone, wouldn't we just...end those relationships? (This argument, of course, excludes relationships that involve abuse and dangerous situations where leaving is unsafe or extremely difficult.) I think after years of writing and podcasting about how much being single doesn't suck, I'm going to be absolutely *aces* at walking away. I'm not afraid to be single; therefore, I'll never stay in a bad relationship just to avoid being alone. It makes me feel powerful.

Until we shed the fear of singlehood, I believe it's more likely we'll rationalize away things we don't like about our partners, slowly building up tiny secret resentments like a collection of human teeth we keep in a drawer, eventually exploding into some unfortunate behavior like throwing all of their belongings off a balcony, nineties-movie style. We can do better than that.

I think we shed fear in two ways—first, by acknowledging that being single has had really bad PR.

Of *course, we don't want to be single* when all we've ever known is we should avoid "ending up" alone like a puddle of cloudy curb water festering in the August sun. If all you've ever been fed is shame, coupled with (purposeful phrasing) outlandish wedding celebrations for people who accomplish the arduous task that is...wait for it...publicly agreeing to continue sleeping with the person they're already sleeping with, you're bound to hold a view of singlehood that's pretty shit.

By now, we know it's my belief that being single isn't a bad, wrong, or shameful thing. This belief is a miracle, when you consider that I didn't really have anyone around to help me see the good parts of being single, or even to see the good parts of myself that didn't deserve to suffer through the misery of hating singlehood. That's probably why it took ten *facacta* years to snap out of it. But at some point in my mid-thirties, I decided I could either keep clawing away at dating apps—convinced by a myth that my husband was hiding in there somewhere, instead of acknowledging that in ten years of online dating, he hadn't been—or I could take a look around at single life and ask myself what was actually so bad. As it turns out, not much.

Freedom's just another word for never sharing the remote control. Honestly, when you stop looking around at how much boyfriend you don't have and start recognizing how much freedom you do have, it's unfathomable to me that anyone still puts up with partners who expect to be taken care of, refuse to talk about feelings, belittle you in public, and let your ass sink into cold toilet water in the middle of the night because they can't be bothered to flip down a fucking seat. If you think being single sounds worse than that, come here and let me hug you.

A whole bed to myself will always be preferable to being with someone I have to bitch at and painstakingly negotiate with more often than I simply exist with in peace. We fear the idea of being single so much that we'll put up with the reality of a relationship that's a genuine struggle. And we don't have to.

Being single is as free, fun, and full as you decide you're going to make it. This is hard to see when you have your head down in a dating app all the time. You're constantly swiping through reminders that you're alone, while wishing you weren't. Of course, you don't like being alone if your life revolves around dating. Dating fucking sucks! When dating is all you can focus on because you hate your singlehood, you miss out on opportunities to show yourself how much more there is to this time in our lives than just searching for partnership.

The second part of shedding the fear of singlehood is a discussion of self-worth. How high is yours? Is yours walk-away-from-shit-you-don't-deserve high? Or stick-around-because-this-is-better-than-nothing low? I guarantee you that you deserve better than "better than nothing." I don't even have to meet you to know that. It's just true.

What does low self-worth look like? Practically, it looks like letting guys you almost dated but really didn't window-shop you on Instagram, because a morsel of attention is better than nothing. It looks like continuing to respond to someone who refuses to make concrete plans with you but might be free for drinks later. And it looks like staying in a relationship that constantly disappoints you but that's better than nothing—in your head. Low self-worth is settling for scraps of attention, and crumbs of what you really want. It's taking what you can get because you're too scared to say no to what's available, however meager. It's being scared that the bare minimum is the most you can get.

I know this is all hard to hear. It was hard to type. But never saying it and never acknowledging it delays our reframing, and I, for one, have waited long enough.

When you have low self-worth, you settle for less than what you want, because you don't think you deserve it—and you don't think you're the kind of person who could have something good come into their life. On one hand, you don't feel deserving, and on the other, you don't believe you'll ever find what you actually want. Deservingness has to come from inside you, but I think I can help you feel better about the finding part. I can't tell you how to meet your partner, but I can show you proof that meeting someone without settling is possible. Even better, you can show yourself.

Think of every couple you know, every couple you're related to, every famous couple you admire. They all met in endlessly different ways, and I guarantee you that none of them are perfect. None of them are ideal and imbued them with more worthiness than you already have. All of these couples aren't together because they're perfect, nor are they together because one of them decided, "Welp, guess this is the best I can do." No, they're together because they fell in love and decided to form a partnership.

It happens, literally all the time. People connect. People find each other. All around you is living proof. Stop seeing that proof as evidence of what you don't have, and start thinking of it as proof of what's possible. Don't just see to believe. See to relax. See to take comfort and confidence in the fact that there's nothing better or more special about all the people currently in couples. They're people, imperfect and human, just like you. Couplehood was just something that happened to them by chance, fate, luck, timing—things outside our control. There's nothing they did or orchestrated to be in a place at a time that was exactly perfect for the purpose of meeting someone. Even after they met, there's no magical key they all possess that helped those chance meetings turn into full relationships. If there were, we'd have heard about it by now with all this internet we have lying around. They were just living their lives, and it happened. Just live yours. If you're not scared of being single, and you know you're worth more than the relationship bare minimum, my guess is you'll live a lot easier.

Being single isn't the worst thing you can be. Far from it. Societal judgments and negativity toward singlehood are lying to you, because someone lied to them first. And anyway, are those judgments doing anything to help? Is a society that judges you for being single also ready and able to introduce you to your partner? No? Then they can all have a seat and be quiet.

When you're happy being single, it's less likely you'll be in a miserable relationship—because being single won't be something you fear, and you'll know you're worth more than a relationship you don't actually want. When you're not afraid to be single, you're invincible.

It's time for me to say goodbye now. I genuinely hope what I've learned, and how I've reframed, can help you do the same. You are worth the effort of reframing the negative, limiting narratives of singlehood, and you deserve to be happy—not someday, not once you're in a relationship, not once you "work on yourself," but *right now*.

I know we've been trained to think finding a partner solves the unhappiness associated with being single. You know what? Maybe it can. (It can't—I'm just trying to give society the benefit of the doubt.) But there's another way. There's a way to end being miserably single, and you don't have to find anyone else first. You can choose to change the way you think about single life, and feel better all on your own. I've made that choice, I'm living it, and I am unrecognizable to the woman I was a few years ago. Writing a book is a *shitload* of work. I wouldn't be doing this if I didn't believe in it, and in you.

Don't wait until you're married to love single life. Singlehood is too good to miss by being obsessed with dating and "finding someone." Singlehood is too free and enjoyable to ignore by being face-down in a dating app for a decade. I should know—I was. Relationships are not inherently better than being single. Giving up that false narrative pays endless dividends. When you wake up to appreciate your freedom, possibility, and a compromise-free life tailored to you, only the right relationships become worth leaving singlehood for. Singlehood and couplehood are equal. One is not better than the other. Sit with that thought for a while.

We will never be more free than we are in this moment, and I don't want us to miss it. I also don't want single women to "accept" singlehood, as if being happily single were some kind of participation ribbon. I want us to live it, celebrate it, and love every single second. We don't have to buy in to the ways people shame us, especially since they're not telling the truth.

I wish you could all see each other. It is my great privilege to see you, all of your smiles and homes and careers and degrees and pets and travels and cooking triumphs and promotions and solo furniture assembly and hobbies and all the ways you find joy. And when you're not doing anything at all, when you're just existing as a valid, whole single woman—that makes me happy, too. I know the world doesn't celebrate our joy the way it celebrates couplehood joy. That doesn't mean it doesn't deserve to be celebrated. If the world has too narrow a view to congratulate you on the things that matter to you in your single life, then throw yourself a party and broaden its fucking horizons.

Some of you are actual *scientists*, did you know that?! I am constantly blown away by all the things we are and all the things we can do. Do not wait for another person to validate you into celebration. Know your validity now, and celebrate everything you consider an accomplishment or milestone—big and small—at every opportunity. Also, turn down a wedding or shower invitation if you need to. You haven't been summoned by the queen; you've been asked to wear uncomfortable shoes and make small talk for several hours. If the friendship can't survive you taking care of yourself, it doesn't need to.

You don't have to date if you don't enjoy dating. Dating is not a prerequisite for finding partnership. Suffering through dating hell isn't required, either. You'll never convince me that surviving the very worst of dating will somehow earn me the very best of love. I've seen too much evidence to the contrary, and I know too many couples who met by accident. Choosing not to toil away at dating like a "second job" is not the same thing as giving up. It's choosing to live a better life and believing that you deserve to meet someone during the course of a life you love—rather than thinking you can only find someone through an exasperating life you hate. And if anyone ever gives you any crap about not "doing enough" to "fix" your singlehood, you send their ass to me.

If you want to date, date! But date because you enjoy it, because it adds something to your life, not because you're trying to solve your singlehood. When desperation motivates you to date so you won't be single anymore, exhaustion and disappointment are likely to follow. Dating shouldn't be a nightmare. There shouldn't be horror stories in such abundance. I really do wish our current dating culture were different, and I'm sorry for what it's become. We don't *have* to date, we get to *choose* to, and a choice you voluntarily make should never bring you down.

Your singlehood isn't something to simply survive. It isn't something you have to "get through" in order to make it to the "real" part of your life, couplehood. Your life is real right now, and I hope this book has played some role in helping you see that. There's a reason I had to say all of this in a book: I wanted it to be yours, to be with you. If you need to revisit the concepts in here, I want you to have the option to pull it off the shelf and find comfort in something designed to provide it.

I was able to say all of this because I *am* you. I lived through it, from my perspective, for a very, very long time. The spectrum of things I've experienced and felt in all the days of my singlehood is wider than my arms can reach, but hopefully within the grasp of my words. This is how I help. I've been as low as low gets, and I found a way to rise higher. I love and respect single women very deeply, and I want to bring you with me.

It was important to me to write this to you while I was still single, because I didn't want the story to end with a relationship as a reward or a "See, I did it—so can you!" moment because I find them profoundly annoying if not condescending and dismissive. I think we deserve proof there are more versions of happy endings for us than that. Also...there is no ending at all. Partnership isn't a culmination of your single and dating life. It's just the chapter that comes next. The day I finished this manuscript, I was still single, and still happy.

My singlehood isn't something I hate. It's something I value. I want this for all of us—to stop seeing singlehood as a problem to cure, and to start treasuring it as something we refuse to give up for anything other than the right relationships. Those are the only reasons to ever give up something so personal, so tailored to us, and so free.

Choosing to reframe singlehood into something good, and something that makes you lucky—not lacking—is not the same thing as deciding to be single forever. Other people's relationships don't have to be unhappy for you to be happily single. The effort you put into dating is not tied to any reward of partnership. Single women are allowed to care about more than dating. Stop saving things for "someday." Do it all, experience everything you want to, wait for no one.

You are not wrong, you are not unfinished, and you are not less. You are valid, worthy, and precious. You are everything. We have the space and the freedom to make our singlehood as full as we want it to be. May our future partnerships—if we want them—bring us joy. And may all our single days bring us the very same thing.

Acknowledgments

Thank you to my late grandmother, Doris Silver Kahn, for taking me to the library. She's the reason I love books, and throughout this process I wished I could let her know it was happening. Maybe the mark of a good grandparent is once they're gone, their grandchildren still know *exactly* what they'd say and how they'd react. I know for a fact that there's someone bragging at a Mahjong table somewhere on the other side in a very stylish jumpsuit. She probably keeps several copies of this in her giant purse and hands them out to people whether they want one or not. *"Take it—you'll read it. My granddaughter wrote it!"*

Thank you to my parents, Stephanie and Todd(les), for being proud of me every day, and for rarely letting a phone call go by without a "When are you coming home?" I think it's important to have people who want you around, who know what the forecast is like where you live (no matter how far away that is), who text you to say good morning, and who call to tell you when something funny happens at HomeGoods. I am a very lucky daughter. I'll come home soon.

Jordan Power, our phone call was the final and strongest push I received to self-publish, following *years* of trying to do things the other way. Sometimes you can know something but still need encouragement. Thank you.

Christene Barberich, thank you for being a champion of my career and growth for the last decade. You didn't have to give me the chance to start what would become my dream career, but you did. Twice. I will never forget that. Also, your book recommendations are very good—please send more.

Kate Rizzo, thank you for seeing so much in me, during a time when I didn't think anyone in the book world would ever see anything at all. Thank you for being someone I never had to convince. I appreciate you.

Dr. Bella DePaulo, Kara Loewentheil, Shahroo Izadi, Dr. Kris Marsh, and Jody Day, thank you all for creating work that has made me (and countless others) feel so supported and valid. It is my sincere hope that everyone who enjoys my work will seek out yours as well. Thank you all for being on my podcast, for being my friends, and for being yourselves.

Jakob, Anto, Kieran, and Matthew—I can't believe a WhatsApp group was almost solely responsible for my sanity during a global pandemic. It's mad, isn't it?

Emily, Julie, and Jay—there are funnier things to say, and making you all laugh is one of my life's great joys, but what I really want to say is this: thank you for always making me feel welcome and wanted in your lives. It means a great deal to me.

Conor and Melody—you never forget me. You never forget to check on me or to acknowledge that I matter to you. This is a very big deal to a single person, and I don't take either of you for granted. You don't know each other, but you have me and the same birthday in common, which always makes me smile. Family is who we choose. I'll leave it at that, and I'll text you in five minutes.

Swathi and Barbara—you two were front row for the "before" me, and somehow you loved that person more than I ever did. I've known you both from the time you were single through partnership, marriage, and now motherhood. There aren't words for how happy I am for both of you. I know I should be proud of myself, and that should be enough, but everything feels better when you are proud of me, too. I used to imagine you'd both be standing next to me when I got married. Now the dream is you *still* standing next to me when we're eighty. That fantasy is, quite frankly, more fun. Thank you for being my people.

Thank you, Clem, for everything. I miss you.

To the dating industry: I see you. I see what you're doing to single women. I see how you're taking advantage of us. You will not simply get away with it, not on my watch. This is my first book. I'm not done.

To every ghost, every asshole, every lewd message sender, every dismissive and degrading human being I ever communicated with in ten years of online and IRL dating: thank you. Thank you for the education you afforded me, for building the foundation of a career beyond my imagination, and for getting and staying the fuck out of my life.

To my readers and podcast listeners, and most especially to every single one of my Patreon Patrons, THANK YOU. You are the most supportive and loving community of all time. You overwhelm me in the best possible way. You make me feel purposeful and loved. Right now, you are holding my wildest dream, and you helped make it happen. I can't wait to see what we dream up next. Thank you for being the reason I go to work every day.

And finally, an unquantifiable thank you to Lacy Phillips, who will know why.

xo,
Shani

ABOUT THE AUTHOR

Shani Silver is an author, humor essayist, and podcaster from Fort Worth, Texas. Her name is pronounced like "rainy" with a "sh." She writes most frequently on Medium as well as on her website, *shanisilver.com*. Her podcast, *A Single Serving Podcast*, launched in April 2019 in the hopes of giving single women content that—for once—didn't revolve around dating, and to support women all over the world in reframing the way they see and experience singlehood. Shani has lived and dated in Austin, Texas; Los Angeles, California; Chicago, Illinois; Philadelphia, Pennsylvania; and Brooklyn, New York. She currently lives in New Orleans, Louisiana. Following ten years of fruitless use, Shani permanently deleted her dating apps in January 2019. She has loved her life ever since.

Twitter: *@shanisilver*
Instagram: *@shanisilver*
asinglerevolution@gmail.com
shanisilver.com
patreon.com/shanisilver

A Single Revolution
3436 Magazine Street #8110
New Orleans, LA 70115

Manufactured by Amazon.ca
Bolton, ON